MEMORY WING

Bill Lavender

Poetry Books by Bill Lavender

A Field Guide to Trees

Transfixion

I of the Storm

While Sleeping

look the universe is dreaming

Guest Chain

MEMORY WING

Bill Lavender

BLACK WIDOW PRESS
BOSTON, MA

Black Widow Press is an imprint of Commonwealth Books, Inc., Boston, MA. Distributed to the trade by NBN (National Book Network) throughout North America, Canada, and the U.K. All Black Widow Press books are printed on acid-free paper, and glued into bindings. Black Widow Press and its logo are registered trademarks of Commonwealth Books, Inc.

Joseph S. Phillips and Susan J. Wood, Ph.D, Publishers
www.blackwidowpress.com

Book and cover design by the author.

Cover photo from the CENLA series by Charles R. Franklin, copyright © 2011 by Charles R. Franklin.

ISBN: 978-0-9837079-0-5

Printed in the United States

10 9 8 7 6 5 4 3 2 1

Acknowledgements

Excerpts from this poem have appeared in *Exquisite Corpse*, *The Pinch*, *The Normal School*, and several online venues.

Many thanks to the first readers—Nancy Dixon, Michael Tod Edgerton, Dave Brinks, Rodger Kamenetz and Megan Burns— whose comments and suggestions were of great benefit to me and to anyone who reads on.

Thanks also to Joe Phillips for initial interest and for keeping faith.

Thanks to Chuck for the wonderful cover photo and for being a lifelong friend.

Thanks and apologies to all those whose names appear herein. Several times I attempted to rename my "characters" out of some vague sense of propriety, but I found that the fictionalized names simply didn't "sound right." It dawned on me finally that the sound of their names contained more truth than any of the stories I could tell; these habits of the tongue and ear may be the only pieces of memory that are not simply reflections of our desire. The past exists not in the conceptual content of the language but in the sounds that are carried forward, variously harmonic and dissonant, like a fugue.

CONTENTS

MEMORY WING

I always speak the truth. Not the whole truth, because there's no way to say it all. Saying it all is literally impossible: words fail. Yet it's through this very impossibility that the truth holds on to the real.

—Jacques Lacan, *Television*

PART I

To my mother on her deathbed

she's facing the wall talking to her dead
mother mumbling at the window snow
rising up outside
wind stirring the drifts

is that you she says and i say
yes it's me and she says momma
was just here just here in the
foyer maybe you saw her and bill

is coming later i think
can you stay a while?
when was the last time you saw him?
was it christmas has it been

that long? and i say i think
it's been at least that long
snow falling outside the window
darkness falling early like that winter in

vancouver i was living on the beach
at the western edge of the land
and one day watched the slate-smooth
lightning-stroked face of a snowstorm

walking in across the bay
wind in our faces full of fury
the green water blown back
froth in the air

and blowing even harder till we thought
we might be in real danger re-
treating to the cabin as the lightning
got close but no sooner

slamming the door than the wind
died so utterly that as
the snow began the flakes
fell straight down and so

quiet you could hear them
hitting the ground the gentle
ticking flakes the size of
your thumbnail three inches

in an hour and again for two more
put a layer of silence
outside the window and i was thinking
schools might close or

something but of course up there
nothing stops on account of
snow and i was out of school by then
and had snow tires on my car

to take me to work at the potato farm
mornings we smoked
big joints in the car on the way
then pitchforked into that pile of potatoes

a hundred feet wide nine hundred
feet long and nine feet deep
the old women on the cull line
reminded me of arkansas mount comfort

the pot-luck suppers third monday of
every month farm women with giant
moles and whiskers on their faces
whole chickens that would fly right into

your mouth and pies and corn on the cob
we'd play hide and seek after
in the dark among the cars outside
and later when we got the nerve

in the cemetery hiding behind
the gravestones
momma's momma and hers and
hers among them

some of the old crypts were crumbling
and we'd dare each other to look in
but no one ever wanted to get that close
and next morning covered with

chiggers my ankles always bloody
my blood mingling with chigger blood
which was dog blood deer blood
my body dog's body my body of the woods

waking next morning in musty sheets
lingering
before being dragged
back to the hell of school

every day what could be worse
riding with pop sick
with fear and fear of what?
failure or simply the jabs

the sullen prejudices envy jealousy
passed from provincial parents
to their progeny raw and
unmitigated like

that time i saw bobby joe
hailey taunted in the cafeteria
by a hundred students
just chanting his name bobby

joe bobby joe bobby joe and
he took it for a long time standing
in line pretending not to notice
bobby joe bobby joe bobby joe

just standing in line
with his tray looking
up looking out the window
bobby joe bobby joe bobby joe

then i saw his mouth begin
to quiver and the quiver
gradually to spread down his
body bobby joe bobby joe bobby

and then the tray with its
saucer of jello its half-pint of
milk and its salisbury steak hit the
floor and tears streaming he ran

out to the delighted laughter of
the rest of the eighth grade
and i wondered how he could
get away with that i wished i

could run away like that without
the hall monitors bothering me
you could legally go only just outside
the door to the pay phone

and there was always a line for it
that was where jerry rommel called
in a bomb scare one day they pulled
us out of class for twenty minutes

we sat on the rock wall across
the street from school then
a single cop car pulled up and the cop
went in and came right back out

with jerry all three hundred of us
watching and we clapped and yelled
after they expelled him
me and johnny went down to his

house he was out of jail he and
his dad sitting on the front porch his dad
in his overalls with a beer and he told us
jerry had called the office from the pay

phone and said there's a bomb in this
here school he said in *this* here
school and the vice-principal just
looked out the door of his office and

saw jerry at the phone and when he
said it's gonna go off in thirty minutes
the vice-principal saw jerry's lips move
and the three of us laughed and

jerry rommel laughed too
and we rode our bikes to the drug
store at oak plaza and walked through
slipping anything that would fit into our

pockets we loved to steal loved it
not because we wanted the stuff
but because we wanted them not to have it
because it felt good to deprive them

of their precious shit
we hated them so
the shopkeepers and yard rakers
teachers police everyone who

had a role who *was* something
and that day he caught me
just as i put my hand on the door his
hand fell on my shoulder

and he said son i need you to
come back to the office with me
and i did trembling a little but i hid it
and he said do you want to take

that pen out of your pocket? and i said
yes sir and pulled out one of
what were surely a dozen miscellaneous
pens in the pocket of my baggy pants

he took it and opened it and said
son what is your name and i told
him bill but for a last name told him
randall because there was a kid i

hated in the neighborhood named
bill randall and i made up a
phone number and the guy wrote
it all down with the pen i'd

given back to him and he said
ok son i'm going to keep this and
if i ever see you in here again i'm going
to call your parents is that understood?

and i walked out head
down so humble and contrite
and we rode home laughing
so hard we almost couldn't pedal

and momma says
she's sorry she apologizes
it wasn't her momma she says
but my aunt julia

who'd been there before I came in
her sister julia who's only been
dead twenty years instead of sixty
momma the youngest of ten

and the last living julia and bryan
and phillip and ralph and garland and maude
and willie and berta and baby anna
all gone to mount comfort now

garland the most recent doddering
and vehement with alzheimers
insulting those who slaved for him
paranoid and bitter loved in

memory only the interminable last
year making everyone miserable
his wife and daughter
crying in their pillows but even that even

that year that seemed it would never
end is over now and garland lies
with his wife and brothers and sisters and
mother and father and uncles and aunts and

grandfathers and grandmothers and cousins
and friends and enemies and people
who pretended to be friends but
were really enemies and people he

thought were enemies but were
really friends lies with them all the same
in the frozen earth under the falling
snow in the cemetery at mount

comfort just over the hill there
outside the window
of the memory wing
where my mother lies talking

to them talking
to me and talking to the
dead and i say yes i figured
it was julia i knew

that was who you meant she was
always mixing up names even
among the living especially mine
jerry i mean garland i mean tom i mean bill

she would say we men of
her life my brother and uncle and
father and me merging into that
image that ghost that every male

name described her father was it?
half-obscured under his hat
in a dim daguerreotype closed in a
locket he who by dint of who-knows-

what sort of uxorious or ruthless
play managed to inherit his wife's
father's farm and raise nine children there
eighty-one acres of hilltop and side over-

looking the little creek
they called hamestring
good water for the cattle and
once upon a time

kids drank it too
momma would cross it
every morning
hopping stone to stone because

it was quicker to cut across the valley
than take the road to the school
the school at mount comfort nine
grades in the little room

same little
room where we went to our
pot-luck dinners iron pump-
handle on the well outside

outhouse in the trees opposite the
church and the cemetery already
fairly substantial the class photo
nineteen o three shows thirty kids

three to fifteen tiered in front of
the building overalled barefoot julia
and maude up front first grade and
third julia looking off

left of camera as if to some
appointment in the
future some
place out of frame

at mount comfort julia and my mother
learned the poems momma read to me
from the hundred-and-one best-loved
at bedtime window open to the

night beetles and mayflies crawling
on the screen and she read the highwayman
the wind was a torrent of darkness
the road was a ribbon of moonlight

forming the words carefully
emphasizing the accents and rhymes
he tapped with his whip on the shutters
and who should be waiting there

bess, the landlord's daughter
plaiting a dark red love-knot
sat on the bed facing away from me
throat pulsing with the words as

outside in the dark the crickets kept
a kind of time with her
and dark in the dark old inn-yard
where tim the ostler listened

his eyes were hollows of madness
but he loved the landlord's daughter
me staring out the window
darkness flecked with fireflies

then look for me by moonlight
watch for me by moonlight
i'll come to thee by moonlight
though hell should bar the way

in the poem things are permitted
that are not at home the highwayman
for example is a thief but also good
the highwayman is forgiven

she loosened her hair in the casement
his face burnt like a brand
then he tugged at his rein in the moonlight
and galloped away to the west

she snores softly now on her back
mouth open face sagged with age
i read my poems to her
and wonder if in her sleep

they strike her pale and metallic
as they do me if what she wants
is what i
want a garland

of words to lie down in
she was more practiced
than i am carefully e-
nunciating each syllable

he did not come in the dawning
when the road was a gypsy's ribbon
practiced at making calm because
struggle tightens the knot

they said no word to the landlord
but they gagged his daughter and
there was death at every window
and hell at one dark window

not history that is not
the fact of it but rather the
way of taking it the screen through
which it enters

they had tied her up to attention
with the barrel beneath her breast
and they kissed her
she heard the dead man say

and so history guides by vanities
and whatever there is to fear and
whatever there is to crave in it irretrievably
lost as soon as it is named

she writhed her hands till her fingers were wet
stretched and strained in the darkness
accumulation and acculturation
occult weaving of stroke upon stroke

she held me rapt
transfixed frozen on the bed
the tip of one finger touched it
she would not strive again

track and trail the words leave
the hunt that came over me
she read to my father too at night
across the hall i could hear them

tlot-tlot in the frosty silence
tlot-tlot in the echoing night
her finger moved in the moonlight
shattered her breast in the moonlight

reading my poems to her
now as she sleeps
do they breach
the rampart or

slip surrep-
titiously through her dreams
through her conversations with
the dead and the living do i in

some slight way control her
past reconfigure her history as language
invades memory to reside there
skeuomorphic outdated residual

carapace of an idiom long ago molted
what evacuated the shell? that
would be history just to situate
the word in its world like

the thread in its fabric filament
filament woven into the fabric
alzheimers is linguistic words suddenly
refusing to come from anywhere

but their farthest beginnings
forsaking their narrative their
memory uncle willie the oldest who'd hightailed it
for california as soon as his legs would get him

off the farm but when i met him beaten
run-down with the shakes his hands
wobbled like a wheel out of balance when he
dealt at the family reunion poker games

he'd whisper to a cousin to get a
shot of old crow in his coffee and he'd
bear down on us kids and usually make
off with our quarters he had

to go to the bathroom about every
fifteen minutes always wore a dingy
suit even at the scout camp where we had
the california reunions we kids slept

in the bunks no doors or windows just screens
and the wind blew the dry sea
air through the night and we'd lay in bed
and tell jokes or sneak out and terrorize the

girls' cabins sometimes we'd get into
willie's old crow if they left the kitchen
unguarded but most of my cousins were
lukewarm about such down-low adventures

i was the yard dog always with my
nose to the ground sniffing out the least
little morsel of euphoria booze or beer or
wine or pills or glue usually it was glue in

those days but i could never get any of the
california cousins to go along
they were too hip probably
already smoking pot or at least could if they

wanted to but they didn't
seem any of them to have the fire in the
belly like me arkansas bumpkin that i was i
was ready to jump right into the sky

some of them lived in l.a. some in
santa cruz and they were all straight as arrows
all except for phillip's kids phillip
was the black sheep the only one

who wasn't a white racist fell in love with
a mexican girl married her and had a v.w. van
full of dark tan barefoot spanish-talking
kids she was a beautiful tough round

woman like a botero vision they ran
a dry-cleaners in watts in the sixties but their
kids were a little younger than us and there
were so many of them they stayed together

and needed no one else i couldn't understand this
alone as i was in my triangle holding the third
corner like a geodesic strut and
i loved the family reunions the poker games

and checkers and swimming and watermelons and
big barbeques cousins all over the place cousins
i haven't seen since since we don't have reunions
any more momma constantly working on meals

with the other women pop sitting lazy with the
men but looking down his nose or preaching
outright the evils of drinking always a teetotaler
always railing about it that otherland of euphoria

like that time momma showed me a drunk
poor old guy stumbling down
the street momma curled her lip
see there he can barely walk see him stumble

i had to sit up to see over the dash this
humanity at its lowest slack-jawed humiliated
guilt-ridden stumbling as if under a great weight
drunken man man alone man left

to himself gets worse and worse pop
always said and this was man
left to himself self to self insensate inchoate
disease-ridden body marked with sin

funny how i talk about you as if you were not
here it's hard to tell ourselves from our
ghosts sometimes i mumble she snuffles
and wakes herself is that you? she says

drunks and old women walk alike
pop said once as we watched julia walking
across the driveway her tracks in the snow
going off in all directions despite the careful

attention to her feet the slow shuffle she was
carrying a flower arrangement she did a lot
of flower arranging picked them from her back
yard in farmington brought them to dinner

instead of food and this to everyone's approval
she was an awful cook childless cantankerous
her husband my uncle douglas died when i was
little and pop scared to death she would

have to come live with us but she managed by her-
self drove her blue ford till she was eighty-five mostly
by dint of everyone pulling to the side of the road
when they saw her coming farmington was a small

town five hundred souls most out on farms after uncle
douglas died pop built a little duplex in her back
yard so she could have some income and then one
evening she called our house and asked momma if

pop had come into her house that day she wasn't sure
but she thought her good brooch was missing
momma hung up on her and fumed around the gall
us fixing up the duplex for her and the gall

of her to make such an accusation and the sisters
didn't speak for a while
after that
pop kept going over there to work

just didn't speak to her when he did and
it blew over as those things always did
and then one day to our astonishment julia
announced she was getting married

willis was his name a widower very
sweet old guy so julia did up the flowers
and for the second time got
married in the church at mount comfort

and off they drove to farmington in her blue ford
and next morning pop and i were un-
loading some lumber working on one
of the rentals when willis came walking

up he was distraught nervous couldn't
stop pacing doesn't it he said doesn't it
say in the bible that marriage is founded
in sexual intercourse? doesn't it say that isn't

that the way god intended? and pop just
shook his head and said i don't know
what to tell you
and willis walked away talking to himself

and later that afternoon pop took
julia to get the marriage annulled
and no one not julia nor pop nor momma
nor anyone at mount comfort ever saw or

mentioned willis again and julia went
on with her life such as it was till
one day pop got a call from a neighbor of hers and
he and garland went over and went in and found

her on the couch dead for several days he told
me about it sat me down we went in he said
then paused she was on the couch pausing again
as if he couldn't say it

she'd been there several days
that's all he said and gave me a look like
i hadn't seen before and i couldn't grasp it
wanted to ask did she stink? was she

a skeleton? i wasn't particularly sorry
not to have to hug her any more as she
smelled of mold and dust and wore a thick
layer of powder and rouge applied in the

dark with bad eyes and had no more
interest in things that interested a kid like
me than i did in flower arranging
but when the boxes of her junk started

arriving at our house for sorting into mementos
yard sale and trash i found a little book called
pegasus over the ozarks university city poetry club
nineteen sixty julia had two poems in it

she'd marked them up in pencil moving stanzas
changing words the ending of one called *new lakes* reads
oh cross their span with bridges wall their
freshness in for along the distant

highway is the sound of marching men
i hadn't known she was a poet and never saw
another but those two poems i still have
the little book at home in new orleans

she used a free verse whitmanian line
unlike all the other entries in the little
anthology but still had to rhyme her
unmarked pentameters I found another

familiar name last poet in the book was
rosa marinoni rosa was the madwoman
who lived down anderson lane in
a little shack on the back corner of her family's

farm she dressed like a gypsy all cheap color
and glass jewels and walked down the dirt
road to our house where the pavement started
to ask my parents for a ride into town

sometimes we took her sometimes
not johnny and me would stalk her house
her shack at the back of the family farm
at the edge of the woods we'd emerge from to

spy on her and then go back me and johnny
as at home in those woods as the rabbits and
dogs knew their paths and secret burrows knew
the bobcat's cave on top of the mountain

cat tracks bird skulls and feathers in the
cave-mouth we sat and smoked cigarettes
for lack of a better ritual
we hunted in the underbrush like

wolves ran down young rabbits and
caught them in our hands just to feel
the frantic heart pumping
and johnny one day pinned a snake

with his foot in the weeds and called me over
it's little i said no its not he said and
i reached down and grabbed the tail
it held to the network of

grass stalks and growth rooted
its head underground i pulled
hard leaned back already four feet
of chthonic body showing until finally it let

itself be taken and the polished obsidian
head came out i fell back and it came
for me striking straightening recoiling
i scrambled to get away yet not let go

of its tail i swung it around it tore at
my shoe finally we subdued it and got it in
a toe sack it fought a few minutes
and then relaxed and

later when the day cooled
we took it out and played with it
the smooth dry body smelling of carrion
it bit me on the hand and we watched

the blood flow and laughed then we got
a limb about nine feet long and draped
the snake on it and carried it
between us down ora drive

housewives came to their doors kids stopped
still on their trikes we walked down the
middle of the street with the staff between us
snake twined around seven feet long and

it crossed the stick seven times the head
hung low tongue darting mouth opening when
anyone or thing approached momma called it
a coachwhip jet black down to the tail where

it faded into red momma hated snakes and wanted
always to kill them every snake was a copperhead
she said until further notice she killed
many a king snake with her hoe working

in the garden weeding
between the rows
my first snake was a speckled king
there was still snow on the ground

where it lay across my path
third grade walking
home down cleveland
then the shortcut through the woods

if there is a god that can do such a thing may he
bless the markham sisters for refusing
to sell the woods that were my mother and my
father the woods that surrounded

rosa marinoni's shack our house and the
bobcat cave the woods where i saw an owl
as big as me gliding through the trees
where the ground is oak leaves

and the roof photosynthetic
canopy tangle of briar and nests
honeysuckle and twigs veining the sky
the old cedar tallest tree in the woods

so many limbs you could climb it like a ladder
ground to very peak and there look
over the top of the trees safe
no one could approach this pinnacle

these the woods where the bearded hermit
lived we never saw him but twice once when our
fire had gotten away from us spreading
frantic through the leaves johnny and me

running from one side of the widening
black circle to the other and suddenly
he was there walking the perimeter with
a wet toe sack swatting at the flames

quickly but calm he never even looked at us
or said a word put the fire out
and walked away into the woods
we hunted around but never found

his cabin i saw pop use that toe
sack trick once we were driving home from
church and saw a grass fire at one of anderson's
shacks the whole family out in the yard stomping

in their boots and overalls pop pulled over
got a toe sack from the trunk and went over
and wet it from their well then he walked along
the fire line spinning the sack put out more in

five minutes than they had in an hour
he left the sack with them got back
in the car shaking his head that anybody
could be so stupid it was

the ball family a big family
living in a three room shack the
old man worked at campbell's soup
walked there every morning

seven miles then there was mrs ball
always at the clothes line and there was
biggest brother david and sister joyce
then jimmy who was my age and a little

girl about four there was one
well for every two shacks old-fashioned
with a bucket and rope and spindle-crank
not even a hand pump

behind the shacks anderson had dug out
a slough that connected to one of his ponds
and that's where he put the outhouses
jimmy and me used to hunt snakes back there

every now and then you'd see a big
moccassin body break the surface of the brown
opaque water sometimes they would swim
in patterns fishing coursing side to side

in the ditch and once in that ditch we
found a fledgling songbird of some sort floating
along tweeting his brains out i leaned out over
the water and scooped him up took him home

momma fed it oatmeal and it lived it turned
out to be a brown thrasher it would
sit on momma's shoulder while she was
at the table and open its mouth whenever she

raised her fork and in the fall it went south
and in the spring came back and laid
a nest full of blue eggs in the rose bush
they all learned to eat oatmeal too

that's how pastoral it was
before the fall or at least it seems so
now with the snow falling and her face
ravaged chin sagging mouth open snoring

silhouette in the gray light of the window
arms at her sides those hands that fed
the bird now swollen wrinkled mottled
like homemade paper and just as fragile

and brittle like that time she took me to meet
the hundred-year-old man
we stopped at someone's house after church and
they introduced me to the hundred-year-old man

he sat on the piano bench gave me his hand
it was blue-veined limp and cold
i didn't know what to say so i asked him
are you really a hundred years old?

he nodded yes and then just sat there
as uncomfortable as me but seemingly
resigned as if knowing no discomfort was
ever cured could only be at best

traded for another dis-
comfort i had wanted to see the hundred-
year-old man but once in his presence i
saw what he had to teach me was not

knowledge but grief and i didn't want
to see the hundred-year-old man any more
and in truth i don't know how much longer
i'll be able to sit here with you lost

in your memories in a land of ghosts
with the snow falling on the cemetery
so quiet and still you can hear the flakes
hitting the ground gray shapes

of men moving among the gravestones
in their caps and coats going about their
duties like when we buried uncle willie
they made me a pall bearer first time i was

big enough it was snowing and cold and we
carried the coffin out of the church and around
back to the open hole made short work of it
because it was cold i never saw

a dead person all your brothers' ceremonies
being closed-casket until phillip fine
phillip my clean-cut friend
not white trash like jimmy ball

or slow in school like johnny
so he was of course
your favorite but only
because you didn't know how he was

out of your sight he was a piano prodigy
but he was also a clepto like me
we'd walk to gibsons after school in junior
high and fill out pockets with worthless

junk and one christmas we made a box
to hold albums we wrapped it up like a present
but there was a slit in one corner it would
hold a dozen records and one night we

filled it up four times in one store
before moving on to another we both had
great collections after that
paul revere and the raiders sam the sham

in high school though we hatched our
biggest scheme pulled the band director's keys
out of his door where he'd left them hanging
got on my honda took them to woolworths

copied every one and then took them back
and stuck them back into the door
we were kings for a little while after that
oddly enough i never once used the keys

it was always him and then the others
we sold them to fine figured out right away
the most lucrative things to steal were
chemistry tests they were multiple choice

the answers just a list of letters easily cribbed
and fine would go over at night
get the test out of the chemistry teacher's
file cabinet and just write down the answers we'd

sell those for three bucks but then
started selling copies of the master
key itself for twenty
and padded our record collections

honestly for a change but then
one day i got called into the office i could see
fine sitting in there with the principal so i knew
to expect the worst went in and sat down

beside him and the principal ben winburn
that little round man with the red face
we called him big ben behind his
back started asking me about the keys and i

naturally said i didn't know what he was
talking about but i'd barely begun to lie when
fine burst into tears and blurted out oh just tell
him the truth they know everything already

and i just looked at him i couldn't believe
he could be such a baby but then i saw they were
lining up behind us all the guys we'd sold keys to
and i knew fine had told them everything

and big ben winburn curled his officious lip
and said bill i'm going to do you a big favor
i'm going to let this go after you all pay for
the equipment that was stolen there was a

tape recorder and a television turned up missing
i breathed a sigh of relief the five of us
could come up with the three hundred bucks
they wanted i don't even remember how i

raised my sixty probably stole it from your purse
but i got it together and turned it in and
when i did the sadistic little fuck told me
he'd changed his mind and we were going to

have to tell our parents and to please ask
you to come see him and that night i
went home sick with dread ate dinner watched
t.v. with the two of you and every second of the

evening trying to get up the nerve to say
something but i couldn't do it finally went to bed
and lay there clenched in terror oh
surely if there is a god he'll be throwing

any adult who ever made a kid feel like that
into the mouth of hell tossing them into
the cosmic trashcan like those caricatures
we drew of them and they confiscated in class

and finally i managed to make a noise
come out of my mouth and told pop
the whole story and after a minute he called
you in and the two of you sat on the foot

of my bed and listened in silence until
i was finished and he said is that it?
i was silent as usual is that it? he said again
because if there's something more and i

find it out later there's gonna be hell
to pay i need to know this is everything
and i said that yes it was everything
and then he said ok then roll over

and he took off his belt and whipped me
while you watched and next day we went in
me and him and sat in front of big ben winburn
and listened to the fat little fuck say

how if we weren't so close to finals i would
certainly have been suspended but since
the stolen equipment had been paid for
they were going to let it go and pop said

what stolen equipment and there began
the long series of lies uncovered that resulted
in more whippings and miserable nights
so many i sort of got used to it

and i remember the night something turned
inside me and the dread and fear finally
let go and in their place the sullen rage
i still nurse and then the stubborn resolve

that i wouldn't be weak any more and so
then when i stole the car and ran away
that time and the cops brought me back
and pop said to get on the bed for your whipping

i said no and he pushed me back and
you lay on top of me held me down and
he took off his belt i kicked him in the gut
and of course he whipped me

all the harder and so that was the way
i turned but philip fine was different after that
incident with the key he turned to god
and not just going to church but carrying

his bible around school and preaching to
kids making little drawings like with
man on one side and god on the other
and the cross as the bridge between them

and i never spoke to him again
except once when he tried to preach to me
i told him to fuck off and then after
high school he did indeed find god went

to oral roberts u. while i was growing my hair long
going to class barefoot and tripping
at rock concerts he was studying to be
an evangelical minister when god took

him up on his offer hit by a truck on his
little honda his first semester there they had
the funeral at the new presbyterian place
north of town on what had been farm land

just two years earlier there was a visitation
the night before open casket that was
when i saw him my first dead person
you cried a little bit and pop

put his arm around you in that way of
his that proffered both comfort and sup-
eriority he liked to say he had an inferiority
complex but he was glad for it

those who felt inferior worked harder and
were more fair to their fellow
man those who felt superior were lazy
and never accomplished anything but

it always seemed to me he acted superior
not inferior and as philip fine lay there in
the open casket he was stoic with his
arm around you and the both of you utterly

utterly ignoring me i didn't feel
much of anything in fact i was surprised
that the sight of his corpse inspired within
me no apparent feeling whatsoever and it

41

wasn't even that i hated him or felt residual
rage from the old betrayal no that all felt
like something i'd grown past i had all but
forgotten about him and now as he or

rather his effigy his crudely made-up dressed-
up carcass looking somehow less real than
the wax figures at madame tussaud's he and
i had viewed together that summer we took

him on our vacation so i would have some
company no there was no nostalgia for any
of that no regret no feeling of loss only a
kind of numb feeling of surreality

as if vision could be anaesthetized in the way
that touch could so that in my seeing him
there was the half-sensation of pressure or
tugging but not the full sense of vision

of touching him with my vision
much less any heightened sense of
my own mortality a feeling that i was half
expecting for at this point as i'd begun reading

the romantics and next day at the funeral
his mother found and hugged me like her long-
lost oh bill oh bill she said clutching
and weeping her tears wet on my cheek

me in my sunday clothes that i hated
and everyone thought the tears i
wiped from my face were mine her
water was warm at first then cooling

on my cheek her spectacled school-marm
face left me cold but the smear of her
liquid on my cheek made me restless
and wanting to get out of there

and then a few years later i
was living in a little hippie apartment
in town and got behind on the electric bill fine's
dad delbert was his name and i'm not making

that up he worked at the electric company and
he called me one day to say that they were going
to have to turn it off if i didn't pay the bill
pretty soon and i thanked him and went

down and paid it and was always grateful he
had called me and not pop because he knew
him of course and then i realized there was
a strange and subtle bond between

almost like we shared a secret
and i realized he'd seen the same
thing in his son's coffin i did
he'd seen the wax figure in his son's place

and delbert and i shared this secret
and we didn't tell pop
and we didn't tell philip's
mother

i didn't have that apartment much longer
got behind on the rent and the landlady
came one day and asked what was up and
i said well i guess i'll just have to move

and you can use the damage deposit to
pay the arrears and she said well the place
is not in that good a condition and i said
you're lucky it's as good as it is like

for example the picture window isn't broken
or anything and she said i'll bet your parents
have a time with you that apartment was half
of a duplex and a couple named claude and kathy

lived on the other side the walls were thin
and i could hear them when they argued
which they often did and one night
it got loud and then the door slammed and

claude was gone for good i was still a
virgin at the time though i would never
have told anyone that and i could hear
kathy sometimes crying through the wall

and there was a closet with a crack in the wall
behind my clothes and sometimes i'd see her
through the crack getting ready for work
ironing her bonanza uniform in her bra

and panties and one saturday afternoon after
claude had left we were smoking and drinking
and listening to music and kathy came over
and got plastered and after everyone else

left i half picked her up and dragged her back
to her side and laid her on her bed such a
nice person she said as she lay back and she
pulled me down on top of her that was

my first time or actually my first three or
four times that afternoon and next day
i went to work at my job at the ralston-
purina turkey processing plant in springdale

it was a wretched job they took the turkeys
clawing and gobbling from the trucks
hung them on a track by their feet and they
started down the line to be killed bled

feathered gutted cleaned frozen boxed
and finally palletized and stored in the big
freezers i worked in boxing thank god
never touched a turkey that wasn't frozen

the guys i worked with were rednecks and
white trash with half pints of sloe gin
and sacks of prince albert in their pockets
and i learned to talk their talk and laugh

at their jokes and we got along fine
but that day seemed like the longest
i couldn't take their racist jokes
didn't want to go out back and smoke with them

i was not in love with kathy but that
day could think of nothing but fucking her
or not thinking it exactly but reliving
refeeling it and a knot of anticipation

formed in my stomach just behind
the navel and tightened till i thought i would
swoon and when i got home didn't even go
to my side went straight to hers she

was sitting on the couch and i said hi
and sat down in the chair across and
she said how was work and i said it sucked
and she said mine too because i kept

dropping things and forgetting what i
was doing because all i could think about
was screwing you and i got up and went
over to her and took her by the hand and

she got up and we walked into her bed-
room and i unbuttoned her bonanza uniform
and dropped it at her feet then she took off
her bra and panties while i got undressed

and we got in the bed and stayed all
afternoon and night i moved out
a few days later and moved back home as
i recall hard to say though it all

runs together time and text
events and things and stories about things
is the past a writing like
this? must we work this hard

to produce it? what about all
that's never been told like when
julia told you i'd been smoking and you
sat me down in the kitchen and gave me

a good talking-to told me stories
about the abject misery of smokers
old men who smoked through holes in
their throats and all the while pop's

talking i can see jimmy ball through
the window over your shoulder he's
standing out at the end of the driveway
leaning against the maple tree like

he always did he would never come to the
door for he knew he was just white trash and we
were rich but he'd lean against that maple
that was covered with

honeysuckle it was jimmy who taught me
how to suck the honey out
of the honeysuckle and he would stand there
and blow through his fists making that great

low pitched whistle and i tried and tried to
whistle like that but never could
but he knew i was in trouble that day and was
just waiting for me to come out

and i told them that i hadn't been smoking
that i didn't smoke that it was all
jimmy jimmy ball had been smoking but not
me and pop said well i really hope that's

true and i went out front and jimmy came up
and said how'd it go and i told him i'd gotten off
easy because i'd lied and told them it was all him
and i figured that would be fine with him because

what did he care what my parents thought
of him? but it wasn't fine with him he got
mad and i said what do you do when your parents
catch you don't you try to blame it on

me? that would be fine with me if you did
blame it on me and he said no i always say
me and bill both did it every time that's what
i tell them and he stood up and for the first

time i was scared of him and he said
that's no good and then he walked out
the driveway and down the dirt road
to his family's shack and he and i

were never friends again and he got
meaner and meaner until he and his
big brother would chase me and johnny
or throw rocks at us whenever we walked by

and that day as i watched him walk away
i knew i'd fucked up but i didn't yet
know the implications and it scared me but
my fear was not fear

of a particular set of events not fear of
losing something but fear of possibilities as yet un-
imagined instinctive reading the
natural sign of his walking away reading

from gesture to gesture without
recourse to language turning his back on
language walking down the dusty road to his
shack i'd hardly been inside it he'd

hardly been in my house either we didn't really
want to go in each others' houses
wanted our life in the woods away from these houses
we met between the houses

and went separately back to them each evening
and if we tried to go inside it didn't work
like once he asked me if i wanted to come see
their new rug and i didn't really but he seemed

excited about it so i said ok and he took me
into their kitchen and said see and i looked
at the floor and saw only a rudely cut piece
of linoleum and was baffled both by the

fact that he would call that a rug and
also that he would be proud of it no matter
what it was called and then one evening
down there sitting in the front yard with

him and his brothers and sisters and some
friends of theirs playing spin the bottle and
i said what's spin the bottle? and they said we'll
show you and they spun and it pointed

to me and big sister joyce came over and
kissed me on the lips and said now
you know what spin the bottle is
and they all laughed and that was

another time i got that feeling in
the gut just inside the navel
that feeling of vertigo
of severance

the game i saw had no strict rules the bottle
was spun and then everyone acted with
a sort of abandon the bottle giving permission
or even mandate to act outside

48

the bounds giddy with transgression
a game with no rule but that the rule
be broken or rules made-up on the spot
to give us something to break

we were always on the lookout
for something to break rules windows
entire houses we'd break in and trash them
rifle through the drawers for cash

open all the little knick-knack boxes
until the house yielded
its secret and every house had a secret
magazines under the mattress a gun

in the bedside drawer old photos of
naked women on a beach all these in
fact were in our house and i'd play
with them when you were gone

pop's army issue forty-five among his under-
wear and socks and those photos from the
south pacific bare-breasted island girls lined
up under the palms the gun was loaded but

i was always careful especially after the time
i was showing caroline the twenty-two showed her
how to cock it then pulled
the trigger and put that nice round hole in

the window you discovered when you came
home that day and then there were the girlie
magazines under the mattress on pop's side the
same magazines johnny and me had hid

out in the woods and other houses had
their secrets too diaries full of confessions
whiskey bottles and cigarettes hidden in
the back shed remember that doctor who lived

on cleveland in the big house with the big yard
and a shed and an old well in the back
with a stone enclosure and a little gazebo
roof? we used to rifle the shed because

we could get to it from behind the bushes
and never be visible from the house but
one time we were walking home from
fourth grade and got there just as the doctor

and his wife pulled out of the driveway
in their cadillac and drove away and then
we walked boldly into the back yard
looked in the windows tried the cellar

door and then we went to the well
lifted up the plywood cover and looked
down to see how deep it was but found
it full to the brim of empty vodka bottles

all the same brand all half-pints thousands
of them we couldn't comprehend
the implications who drank them? why
were they in the well? we picked some

up turned them over a drop or two
in the bottom of each we could have mined
them for a buzz but it was too
weird we thought there might be some-

thing wrong with them some sort of
poison or germs so we left them there
in their mystery and went back
to the street jimmy ball was out there

fighting a kid two years older than him
and way bigger and beating the shit
out of him had him down on the ground
and dropped onto him knee into kidney and

the kid's eyes rolled back in his head
we walked on down cleveland street
and at the bottom of the hill johnny
turned off to the right to go home and

i cut off through the woods to the left
this was the path through the woods that
jimmy ball took home and when i looked off
through the trees and i could see the yeti

man-shape covered with reddish-brown hair
moving along beside me
and it didn't even matter
that i knew he wasn't real still i started to

run and i ran along and every so often would
see something out of the corner of my eye
that i knew was him and then i heard something
in the bushes like i'd spooked an animal

and a javelina broke out of the
brush and ran along beside me and then my dog
tex came out of the woods and joined
me on the other side and the three of us ran

along the path till we came upon a coachwhip
lying across and quick as black lightning
it flashed and ran the path in front of us like
he was our guide like he was the apex of

the triangle and we four ran like that all the
way to the house and we looked back out
the window and could see the yeti peeking
out from the edge of the wood waiting

for when we should have to come back again
and sometimes at night i'd get spooked
lying in bed thinkin about jimmy ball thinkin
about the yeti thinkin about the javelinas

running in the woods the woods the woods
were my best friend and they were the
scariest place they were where i hid and they
were what i hid from and then the wind of the

wing of something
passed over the house in the night
a tornado afar off a great
roar like would shake the world but

miles away on the other side
of the mountain other side of
the bobcat's cave
and the mountain leaned over

leaned and let the bobcat
touch the house
as i lay dreaming
the yeti coming

i dreamed the rabbit in his burrow
dreamed the big cat in his lair
big cat i'd never seen except in dreams
i dreamed the darkness sliced through

itself in planes trying
to make sense of things
and what i'd let go
dreamed johnny and

jimmy ball were friends
dreamed the tornado came over the mountain
bobcats and javelinas ran before it
i dreamed the owl came to my window

i dreamed the coachwhip was in bed with me
and its head disappeared in my navel
i dreamed that when joyce ball bent over
to kiss me she had three eyes

i dreamed the gars in the trees were
swords in the hands of knights
i dreamed i woke up and the pillow
was a sack full of bones

i dreamed the swaying trees were soldiers
coming over the hill
i dreamed i went before a judge
and the judge was a black man

i dreamed whatever i dreamed
came true i dreamed i woke up
and then woke up again i dreamed
i came upon a car wreck and pop was in it

but i snuck by without him seeing
and woke up again with those queasy
innards and on the way to school i told you
my stomach hurts and it did drawn

into a knot behind the navel clenched
fearful which you knew because you said oh
you're just worried you won't find your
seat or something but i knew

where my seat was knew the classrooms
and the halls knew the stairways and the
cafeteria the bathrooms and the playground the
playground with its joy and its terror

knew the teachers knew the kids big and
small knew the principal who called you
when i knocked my teeth out in short knew it
all knew it all already that feeling wasn't

from not knowing where my seat was
but from knowing it too well and it was in
fourth grade i found myself in my seat found
as it were my voice in my seat smarted off

to the teacher for the first time and felt the
approbation of the teacher miss white
but there was something else too something
else there to know and feel as the other kids

turned in their seats and laughed
they laughed at miss white
they laughed as if i'd bested her
and they looked at me and i saw the

future in their eyes saw i would be
the smart ass that i'd know what to say
and say it i'd be smart and also smart
i'd tell them what they didn't know they'd said

turn their own words on them capture
their contradictions and make them a
laughingstock and what did i care if
the entire adult world shook its finger and its

switch at me i and anyone else would have gladly
traded the scorn and indifference of that world
for the rest of our lives for just one afternoon
as king of the playground for we hated

your world loathed it
feared it and never knew
bound to it not by love
not by patriotism but by depth of

our hatred how it commanded our focus
drew out of us the rocks we threw at its windows
guided our hands as we marked up its walls
called us to attention as we pissed on its floors

we said the pledge of allegiance we
set fires and made bombs we put firecrackers
in mailboxes dropped bricks onto cars
from the overpass *dulce et decorum est*

to die for the country pro patria
to die for the father-
land on the pyre of the father
with our m-eighties and our cherry bombs

our twenty-twos and b.b. guns and
the poor sparrows we practiced on
once walking in the woods i heard a crack
nearby and saw the bullet pass

just in front of me through the honey-
suckle i froze and dropped to the ground
said nothing made not a sound for the
instinct of the hunted is to be silent

and knowing discreetly knowing then all
that i have learned since
that there are no accidents no mistakes
i lay on the ground sun shooting through

the dense foliage pencils of light bits of dust
and leaf still floating down from the invisible
line of the bullet imagining that line
going through me belly-button to kidney

like years later when johnny took me over to this
new kid's house wendel was his name and we just
went there and knocked on the door and his mother
opened it and we said is wendel here? and she said

yes he's back in his room and we went through
the living room with the shag carpet and down
the hall to his little bedroom and he said
what are yall doin? and we said not much and he said

who are you? and johnny said i'm johnny and that's bill
and wendel was sitting on the bed and he drew
his left knee up to his chest and pulled up the leg
of his jeans and pointed to a round scar the size of

a quarter and said see this? that's where i shot myself
and then he showed us the exit scar on the other
side and held his two fingers one on either side
so we could see visualize the path the bullet took

a twenty-two is so small it makes a hole about the size
of a pencil so it was like a pencil went through
his leg my stomach tightened and i said damn
but he said what? ain't no big shit and i said

why'd you shoot yourself? and he and johnny
both laughed and said he didn't do it on purpose
stupid and he said i was just layin on the bed
fucking around with the rifle and shot myself

in the ankle by accident and i said ok let's go
somewhere and he said ok and we went out to
the living room and he says to his mom can i have
some money? and she said that's up to your father

as his dad sat impassive behind his paper and
wendel went up to him peeked over the paper
and silently mouthed money and the old man
said to his wife well do you think he's earned it?

and she said no i don't think he's earned it but
i don't think it would hurt anything to give it
to him and the old man just grunts and keeps on
scowling at his paper as wendel's mother gets a

couple of bucks out of her purse for him i didn't
see much of wendel's parents after that but
i remembered the scowl on his old man's face
when we got arrested for the third or fourth time

standing at the counter at the jail waiting
for the cops to call our parents one at a
time first you because they knew pop's name
then johnny's and then when he dialed wendel's

house saying mister orand this is fayetteville city
police we have your son and then moving the
phone away from his ear it was so loud
all of us heard his old man yell leave him there

and the cops hanging around the desk all
started laughing and saying well son i guess
you're gonna be here a while and wendel
giving his shit-eatin grin and saying yeah

i guess i will and when pop came to get me
i told him what wendel's dad had said thinking
that maybe pop would bail wendel out too
but he just said well it's what he deserves ain't it?

we oughta leave all of you there
but as we were pulling out of the parking lot
another car was pulling in and i recognized
wendel's old man's scowl when we caught

him in the headlights so all three of us went
home to our whippings i imagine though
we never talked about such things we were
not interested in each others' home lives

beyond the occasional pang of jealousy that
one or the other of us got a punishment less
severe or a toy more expensive we only cared
about what happened when we were alone

away from adults outside our suburban brick
and though we had pool tables and
electric trains in our basements
we met each other under bridges

in abandoned shacks and lean-tos in the woods
we had places all over town like under the overpass
on lafayette or in the big culvert where the creek
went under the road in front of anderson's field

once walking that creek we found a network
of tunnels dug into the bank we were mystified
thought maybe an animal had done it but they
were human-sized like big enough for us to crawl

around in so we figured it must have been boys
like us who dug them but they were so elaborate
and extensive it must have taken them weeks
way more work than we would ever have devoted

to such a project but we were impressed crawled
in one and came back out and lay in the opening
three heads sticking out the creekbank
and we came back to the tunnels a lot

then one day came there to find jimmy
ball's big brother david on the bank
sand was flying out the holes at a pretty
good clip and when we came up

david ball said we got company and three
of his buddies came crawling out
they had camp shovels and were covered
with dirt and sweat and david ball said

you little shits been messin with our tunnels
ain't you? we knew somebody'd been here
and we're gonna kick your ass
we ran for it and we got away actually

they let us go for they were in high school
and could easily have caught us
and after that we'd always sneak up on the place
making sure they weren't there before

we showed ourselves and then one day we
came and the tunnels were gone
the holes in the bank closed up like eyelids
and the network now a network of

ditches in the field up top and at the end
of one ditch was a hole and in the bottom of that
hole was one of their camp shovels
still perfectly good just caked with dirt

and momma snuffles and opens her eyes
rolls her head toward me and says shovel?
yes i say though i didn't think i was speaking
out loud they left it? she says and i say

yes they left it i don't know why and then
because i know how she is about
not letting anything go to waste saving everything
in case it might be needed one day

even though it isn't true i say
me and johnny took it and kept it and that was
our camp shovel from then on it was what
i used in boy scouts and any time i went camping

you saved it? she says and i say
yeah we saved it
and i am waiting for her to speak again
but the next sound she makes is a snore

we had indeed taken the shovel with us
hid it in the woods for when we might
need it then forgot about it i came upon it
years later the handle rotten

the iron rusted permanently in its hoe position
she would have cringed
then nodded sadly for
what i know

i know from her lips
every other word seemed
some lesson about time getting away
some lost opportunity or regretful misstep

or how smart and beautiful so-and-so was until
she grew up to be a teenager and grew
her hair long and refused
to wear make-up she could make

the wretched privation of her past
sound like a lost heaven a world of
teeming nature and harmony
where the dog would always come

to your rescue and the horses were
as smart as whips or she might see
hush-puppies on a plate and tell
about the time she and her momma and

sisters got stuck on the road in a broke-
down wagon and they stayed the night
in a friendly neighbor's barn and there was nothing
to eat but a sack of corn meal and her

momma made corn dodgers and they were
the best thing she ever ate
though the funny thing was that as she got
older and more and more behind her

she told fewer and fewer of these stories
of the past like after pop died she just
sort of stopped and in the places where
she used to tell them she would go silent

and look out the window
she'd look out the window even
if it was night and there was nothing
to see there but her own reflection

and i'd see her doing that and feel that
knot in my stomach and there was only
one time after he died that she said something
she said i guess he was about the smartest

man i ever knew he could do just about
anything like
concrete
and saying the word as if the beginning of

a list she let it trail off instead let concrete
stand for all his many skills
welding carpentry electrical plumbing
roofing flooring sheetrock insulation whatever

concrete was for her the crowning achievement
the symbol that he could do anything
he got me a job one summer in high school
running the construction of doctor ed wheat's cassette

tape ministry in springdale we were to
add a twenty-five hundred foot
split-level extension onto his doctor's
office to be the tape library and he showed me

how to build the forms for the floor
over the basement i'd never formed
and reinforced a floor like that before
and he said cut all the two by four posts

the same length just a little bit short
and then cut you some wedges and then you
go along and level each one and you'll
get it just as flat as can be and

don't worry if the plywood isn't
laying right when that concrete
gets on it it'll lay right down yes
sir it'll lay right down

so i built the whole cassette
tape ministry building in springdale
with pop just coming by now and
then and for help dr. wheat would give me

a new volunteer or two every week boys
my age but come to do their service
to the church rather than saving
for a motorcycle like me they were

easy to corrupt and they'd smoke
with me out back and then they'd go
check out one the tapes from the library
and come back next morning saying they'd

quit smoking now for good
me and johnny used to love to fuck
with kids going to church we'd ride
by on my honda on sunday evenings

and see kids hanging out out front
and we'd yell church! and slap our knees
and laugh and they'd make a show of being
bad like flip us the bird or pull out a pack

of cigarettes and it was all a joke
since we as you know had to go
to church too but at least not usually
on sunday evening the morning i was

resigned to but when you made me go
at night that seemed way too much especially
if johnny didn't have to though
there was that one time you made me

on a sunday night and the preacher got up
and said i have taken the liberty of inviting
so-and-so who is visiting from someplace
to give the sermon tonight i'll

let you tell me if i have made the right
decision and this pudgy little guy came
hobbling up to the pulpit he slid his feet and
looked off to the side and jerked his head

his face was soft and flaccid like a baby's
and he started to talk and i thought
man this is fucked up because
you could barely understand he slurred

his words so like he couldn't control
his lips and his tongue and he talked
on and on and then i heard and you just
take a minute to tune me in and i think

you'll understand after that and the funny
thing was i did and the way he talked
began to seem more and more normal
and then suddenly it was not only under-

standable it was as clear as anything
i ever heard and the rest of the crowd
and the church and the sunday evening
seemed to fuzz over until all i could

see or hear was him in a little circle
at the center of my vision
and he told a story about how he was
born with cerbral palsy and learned

early on not to expect things to go
well for him that he was afflicted and would
never lead a normal life but then one
night he chanced to enter a church and

there accepted jesus christ as his
savior and after that he prayed to jesus
that he could have a job so that he could
support himself and not be a burden on

his foster-parents and sure enough right after
that a guy called and had a job that he could
do and he has been self-sufficient ever since
and then he prayed for other

things like education a place to live
etc. and every time his prayer was granted
and then finally he said one night he prayed
oh sweet lord that has given me so

much and so much undeserved forgive me
that i might have the pride and wanton
arrogance to ask such a thing but i ask it
only as i know with all my heart of your great

generosity and i know i am not worthy
of the gift i ask for and if you do not see
fit to grant me this most presumptuous
request it will not make any difference to me

i will still love thee and serve thee all
the rest of my days but should you in your infinite
grace see fit to grant me this you
will have shown yourself more ben-

evolent than even your most devoted
prophets have proclaimed and this one
request that i have is that you might send
me along with all your other bounty a wife

that i might procreate and have healthy
children and teach them to praise your name
and then he said that god sent him
the most beautiful and charitable woman

any man had ever known
and everyone in the congregation sat
transfixed it was as if rays
of light emanated from the pulpit

and people started saying amen or praise
but their voices sounded strange like they were
speaking an alien language only his
voice sounded normal now and the men

in the congregation began one by one
to go to the front where they knelt
on one knee and bowed their heads
and pop went down there and some of the

kids my age but enthalled as i
was i did not want to join the group
and the women didn't go down either
neither you nor anyone else and i

didn't know if it was because this preacher
with cerebral palsy didn't affect women
the same way he affected men or if women
just didn't feel that spiritual

ecstacy the men felt even though they
all said how great a preacher he was
after the service we went about as
before us kids playing outside in the

parking lot while the adults filed
slowly out we had found that the obscure
glass window on the women's rest-
room wasn't as obscure as it was supposed to be

and we'd huddle outside it and watch
the staid old church women and some of them
not so old come in and hike up their
skirts and pull down their pants

and we'd snicker at the pubic hair
and put our hands over our mouths to keep
the laughter from being heard
and then one night a few

weeks later one of those sunday evenings
me and johnny had been out on the bike
you and pop came home and gravely told me
that brian and his brother had been discovered

peeking in the women's bathroom
and i wanted to laugh but both of you looked
so serious i just said wow and pop said
there'll be a special meeting of the elders

to decide what to do with them but tell
me this because i need to know and i need
to know the truth did you have any idea
this was going on? and i of course said no

and of course instead of just putting up
a curtain and going on with business
those two kids were brought before the
elders made to feel sick or dirty and me to feel guilty

for not being punished with them
even pop had his photos with the deckled
edges of the bare-breasted native girls
in the dresser drawer you knew that

but everything at church had to have this
high seriousness and drama about it
as if some little infraction like that was
a kind of treason it was like

something out of sade
massive punishment for a minute
and arbitrary transgression
the body and its noises do you

giggle or frown when someone farts?
depends on the context doesn't it?
and that church was a context that
protested too much had its own

undercurrent of weird sex
pederasty infidelity ecstatic preacher-
fucking i knew all about it knew the
preacher's kids knew the reason for the rule

that preachers' kids are always the wildest
like carl would always entertain us
with stories about his sexual experiences
or those of close female relatives

he was about twelve at the time and me about
ten and he told me how he'd walked
in on his sister going at it with a hot dog
and how she tried to hide it under her

skirt but it fell out on the floor and he said
ah sis why you doin this why don't you go
out and get you some real dick? and after some
discussion she realized the wisdom of his

words and went out and got some
and now she knew what was up and it would be
easy as hell for me to get some of that
if i wanted and i said are you nuts? but

secretly connived to be alone with her
though once there i'd get nervous and
blush and stutter and she'd look
at me like i was crazy i remember

these scenes quite vividly sometimes
everything but myself in them as if
there were an empty place
and i am looking out from there

sitting at one of those
tables in the old union stoned me
and cannon and mike and feeling that
welling up inside heat emanating from

the groin hard and pushing against my
jeans panting about as obvious as
hands between my knees and cannon
leaning on his fist looking over

at me eyebrows going up into a
question mark thinking about it
thinking and not thinking
too much crowding in at once

and looking away thus missing
my chance with that particular
lord of this life and remembering
that afternoon at marian's

house me and marian and wendel and
kay on the bed my mouth on marian's
her jeans unbuttoned fingering in her
bush afterwards me and wendel trading finger

sniffs oh you got some of that too did you?
and talking that very afternoon about leaving
making the plan and the date i lay
in bed waiting for you and pop to doze

you were reading to him an animal
story of some kind i'm sure some reader's
digest adventure of a dog who'd lost his way
and makes it home against terrible odds

i could hear you faintly across the hall
on and on until finally the familiar
snore catch yourself snore and i got up
and tiptoed shoes in hand down the

stairs to the carport got in the buick
started it backed out without any lights then
cruising down the road lighting a cig-
arette because what the fuck did it matter now

if we smoked in the car? kay was on the corner
like she said she would be and wendel on his
front porch but marian did not show and we
drove around drove by her house all

dark then parked down the street and
waited for an hour or so kay and wendel making
out in the back seat and after that we figured
we better go so we drove out drove all

night to kansas city woke up the next morning
to a guy knocking on the window telling
us we'd get a ticket for parking the wrong
direction there and that was new to me i'd never

heard of getting a ticket for parking the wrong
direction so i moved the car and we sat
around for a few hours drinking cokes and
doing nothing then we drove back to

fayetteville stopped at the stop n shop and called
marian on the pay phone and she said
where are you i'll meet you
and she drove out in her dad's

car and parked and got in with us and said
she couldn't come last night because her
dad caught her and anyway she wasn't
sure it wasn't for the best wasn't it

for the best? and didn't i know
that she cared and only wanted the
best for me and everyone and then she
got out of the car and went back

to hers and suddenly i understood and
gunned it around the corner but there
was the sheriff already across the road
and the second car pulled in behind us

and that little squirrelly wanna-be boyfriend
of marian's junior deputy riding
in the second car with the real cop
and they put me and wendel against the

car spread our legs all their idiotic
posturing and took us down to the courthouse
basement the old courthouse all white-
washed sandstone the fat old sheriff

sitting at his desk and he talked to us a few
minutes and then he nodded to wendel and
said i want him mugged and i thought
that meant they were going to beat him up

but all they did was take his picture
and mine too kay's daddy came down all
blubbering tears and wrapped her in his pallid
arms and took her home and pop

and you came for me took me home
for a whipping asking if i had had sex-
ual intercourse with kay and then saying with
rising voice that i could be guilty of crossing

a state line for immoral purposes
it was gonna be reform school if i was
lucky but of course we never heard from the
heat again it was their own car after

all so we all moped around for a few
days but it was ok i barely heard
from marian again we heard her parents
took her to a gyno and had her checked and

the gyno looked at her and she said once
a long time ago and he said yeah and a
lot of times in between that was the story that
she would fuck anybody anybody that is i

guess but me and pretty soon after all that pop
came into my room and said we need to build a
hay barn for your horse and we went up into
the woods by the little shed where we kept

her grain and saddle and he took a twelve
foot one by four and had me stand on one end
while he walked the other end around in a
half circle and every so often he drove a stake

in the ground and then we took that same
old one by four that'd been used ten times
previous for everything from batting to
a concrete form and we bent it around the

arc and put a small nail in each stake then
we put another one and a third till we were
all the way around then we came back with
another one on top of that spacing

the second so it lapped the joints of
the first and then a third and then
a fouth layer nailing the last one on pretty
good then we pried it off the stakes and

propped it upright
braced it off then built the second then
the third put them on three foot centers
nine of them for twenty-seven feet then we

plumbed up the ends and ran sleepers
between them on two foot centers
covered the whole with tin took less
than two days to finish it and

we kept sandy's hay in there from
then on along with other stuff he wanted
to keep dry sacks of cement and insulation
and such a quonset hut he called it i found

a ribbon snake in it once its red
and yellow flash among
the dun of the hay and once
when i came to give sandy her

grain a coon was into it and i was able
to drop a wash tub over him i
put a hay bale on top of it and went
to get a cage came back took the bale off

lifted the tub and as i started to think
just how i might be able to get that coon
into my cage the coon never even
concerned himself just walked no hurry

at all out the front of the hut stopped
in the opening looked back at me in that
impassive poker-faced way coons look
me bent over holding up the tub in one

hand and a chicken wire cage in the other
trying to read the robber mask
before he turned and
went on into the woods

pop built us a shed out of scrap too a shed
in the woods for me and caroline to play in
out of old shiplap and four by fours and then
years later pop and me go up there to tear it

down so we can reuse the shiplap and inside
they had written all over it and drew pictures
stuff like bill fucked caroline we seent him fuck her
and pictures of stick-figures fucking

wrote all over it in colored chalk on each one
by twelve board there was a sentence so that
when we took each board it was like
carrying a sentence to the truck and pop

of course never said a word just
careful to put the writing side down
and though there was nothing for
me to fear from these statements

just being in their presence with him
just carrying them silently between us
shamed me reminded me of everything
we had to carry silently between us

of course i didn't fuck caroline i was in the
third grade she in the first what sort of
fucking were we supposed to have done?
she seemed to be anxious to grow up

having witnessed perhaps some scene some
moment of grown-up behavior that left her
allured yet mystified by physical apparatus
and the various postures and we'd spend afternoons

in the shed examining each other
one laying down legs spread the other
peering probing like a doctor
i remember being surprised by the precise

position of the anus and marvelled
at its ingenuity when a turd peeked out
like a little black eye the sphincter swelling
around it quickly until it was born and lay

forlornly on the dirt floor of the shed
and she taught me it's true how
to fuck told me to put my tiny white
thing against hers which i did dutifully

standing up sticking our
torsos toward each other cooly
touching pasty white flesh to flesh
for a moment and then looking around

pulling up our pants standing awkwardly
we called it our hobby let's go
do our hobby she would say every
morning when she came up to my

73

house until finally one day i told her
i didn't want to do our hobby any more
she was crestfallen she was starting to
cry so i added quickly well just not every

day i mean we can still do it sometimes
but i don't think it should be our hobby
and she sniffed and then smiled and said
you're right we don't have to do it every

day from now on it won't be our hobby
but just like a second hobby and our first
hobby will be well i guess it should be
climbing trees i like to climb trees

and so do you so from now on when we
say let's go do our hobby that will mean
let's go climb trees and if we say let's go
do our second hobby that will mean let's go

fuck and we'll just do that every now and
then and i said ok and she said ok let's go
do our hobby and we went out in the woods to
the big cedar with a branch every foot like

a ladder and we climbed up into it and
looked out over the tops of the other trees
in the woods and she had two cigarettes she
had gotten from her parents and we

smoked them and when we went back
down we picked some honey-
suckle blossoms pulled out their plungers and
drank the honey from them

then she said want to
go do our second hobby? and after that
never mentioned our first hobby again
just came every day and said let's go

do our second hobby ok? she moved
away pretty soon as i remember but there
was that one evening i was out by the barn
just in the grass where i could see her

house and i was playing with the dog
i think since there were no other kids right
then for me to play with and i was
hoping she was going to come out but

then i heard her father yelling
her name caroline c. smith! he yelled
and from his voice you could tell he had
caught her in some shameful act or

found out some sordid truth about her
i went on playing with the dog but we
edged back a little closer to our house
caroline moved away right after that

momma said they were trash and she
called them the ritters which i thought was
strange because her father called her
smith and i had the strange idea that her father

called her that as a way of saying she was
as common as a smith and i thought of that
again when i was in sixth grade with two
linda smiths and i noticed how

they were different but also the same
not sisters even more alike than that
and we'd walk home every day all of us linda
smith linda smith johnny kay jimmy ball and

me and one time jimmy ball says hey remember
that little girl caroline used to live up by you
what ever happened to her she used to come
around every other day and want to fuck so

did you fuck her? i said
shit yeah i fucked her he said
all this past
and future carried on

the boards between me and pop that
day we used those boards for siding
on one of the duplexes he was building
and they're still there now and maybe some day

some guy'll tear that siding off and when
it lays down he'll see those sentences
and he won't know who caroline or bill was
but maybe he'll feel the silence we

carried between us and faced to
the wall for fifty-six years he'll know it
because it is the silence we all carry imagine
me on one end of that board and me

on the other end too and that's the way it
is the awkward silence of right now
can't say a word can you? he would say when
i was in trouble over something and getting

the talk can't look me in the eye and can't
say a word can you? no but i know the look
of the floor the asbestos tile with its smeared
pattern the thin mahogany

baseboard the gray plastic cups
on the chairs' feet the rough edge where
the tile met the mortar of the hearth and inside
the ashes the stone darkened with

smoke it smelled of smoke even
in the summer the mantle of rude arkansas
stone at a height where one could lay an
arm on it with one foot on the hearth and

address the room with napoleonic auth-
ority after supper or as occasions demanded
stern or joking or quiet with some sobering
object lesson of the day while we the

audience sat and looked on stone of the
fireplace for backdrop the darkened fire-
box still entrancing once as i sat watching
came a commotion of falling black

dust and stuff and behind it a
bird
coming into the room on a fury
of flapping wings trail of dust in the air

you said it was a swift and
i ran around crazy trying to
catch it careened around the front
room bouncing off the windows

getting behind the curtains i was
right behind it and felt the gray
feathers flutter in my hand once or
twice then finally trapped

him in a corner of the window frame
pulled back my hand only the bird's
head sticking out panicked panting
heart aflutter the worthless little

beak biting sideways at my finger
and i wanted to keep it but you said
let it go they keep the chimney clean
so i took it outside and threw

it up in the air where it
shuddered stumbled then caught itself
pulled up into the red oak
disappeared among the foliage

the creek that came down the
back yard ran under that
red oak widened there
to form a pool blackened by leaves and

when it rained the creek would run a
torrent and spread out into the yard below
taking the leaves and crawdads and tadpoles
and most of the gravel driveway with it

at night i mulled its motion the slick
calm the ripples from a falling
leaf and then the sudden roaring
current that emptied the pond and left

things flipping in the grass
black pond under black air
electric charge in the atmosphere
it opened down like a well

like the well me and
johnny looked down
saw our faces in the bottom
looking up out of a porthole

and something moving
rippling the water
a garter snake swimming around
the edge butting its nose

against the slick stone wall of the shaft
looking for a purchase
for a head-hold we dropped
sticks down at it saw our faces waver

like ghosts and then something
grabbed us lifted us kicking and
yelling off the ground
the hermit had us by the nape

and we'd fouled his well he tossed us
down in the grass like trash
and walked off in his dirty overalls
long scrappy hair like a forest

yeti like a guardian
of the woods and we went down
and hid in the bobcat's cave
crouched shivering holding onto

our knees until night fell and the mouth
of the cave was like moonlight
reflected in a pool and we
heard the bobcat coming over the leaves

saw the yellow eyes
looking back from the cave's mouth
looking up from the pool
and there was nothing to do but

go on in deeper and we crawled
hands and knees it was
cold and the ground was wet
and never was there dark this dark

i felt the way along the stone
the path grew narrow the ceiling
fell and panic hit me the raw searing
terror that claws from the deep

and i struggled to turn around but
johnny said no we can do it just
relax and next i knew the ceiling opened up
and we were in a great room

standing up and raising our arms felt
around us and felt nothing
and then a slight
shudder in my knees the floor

dematerializing by degrees
i floated free
for there was nothing
in space by which i might

check my motion
johnny's call to me sounded
near then far high pitched then low
young then old and i struggling

to relax to remain still but
panicked flailing in vacuo
and my movement was
of no consequence my terror

stirred not a ripple on the
chthonic waters
in the great well of darkness
under the hermit's shack

she stirs now
snuffling in sleep
mumbling
at the window

snow rising up beyond it
whirlwind of souls
is that you? she says
momma was just here

and i say ah and she says
what was that you were
saying? and i say oh it was
nothing i was just reading you

a poem a poem she says then looks
away moving her lips as if trying
to remember something digging back
deep for the words trying them

on her lips as if to say are these the words
i was searching for? how does that poem
go again? i half hear an echo of the phrase perhaps
if i move my lips the sound will

remember itself there rhyme and rhythm
move through me make the words i have
forgotten come from my throat
a funny feeling in my throat

like that morning i was about five rubbing
sleep out of my eyes i wanted to tell her
how my throat felt
my throat's ken i said

the word spoke itself and
when it did i knew where words
came from how they arose directly from the things
they described tree called itself tree

plate plate water water going going
they were precise and irrevocably connected
required no definition rather their
sound alone said them as clearly as could

be said but then she said what?
and laughed a little at my cuteness
what do you mean ken?
and i was embarrassed and didn't

trust my words after that kept my autospeech my
speaking in tongues to myself
at the pentecostal holiness
down the road from johnny's we'd watch

through the window as they
stood in the aisles and talked like that
i went to catholic school though
because my birthday was in october

81

and the catholics would take me when
i was technically still five i'd never
seen a nun before being abandoned to
sister marietta to learn my alphabet

and then my phonics at which
for some reason i excelled
saint joseph's the school was called
where once i brought in

for show and tell
a honey locust branch
with the longest thorns i'd ever seen
for i thought it a wonder

but a kid named rock
asked for it
and i gave it to him
because friends were

hard to come by at st joseph's
he ran around at recess
poking his pals in the butt with the
three inch thorns and them running and

jumping like cartoon victims i watched
from the swing learned to pump it higher and higher
the science of it came to me i understood how
if i swung beyond horizontal a moment of free

fall would begin and then
end with a jerk halfway down
i loved the swing and its vertigo
loved to push myself out at its high point

and land in the grass ten feet out
i was a jumper jumped
out of trees off the jungle gym
jumped off of the roof of the shop into

the big sawdust pile at the back
and you could jump into it and down
deep in its heart the sawdust was
warm and somehow i knew that

was natural too something in sawdust made
heat and that was right and normal and if i'd
thought about it beforehand i
would have known it and all things

science all things of the world seemed
that way to me logical wound in truth
like a bell ringing
truth in the simple sound of it

electricity i sensed
with first encounter with the d battery
buzzer and telegraph switch in fifth
grade immediately its logic of the continuous

path and later understood the scent trails
of ants in the same way in either case
you could throw the switch and turn off
in one case the buzzer in the other

the orderly passage of food to the
queen and then in one incident learned
a cover-all-bases approach to electricity it was
christmas break the campus

empty snow-covered pristine and silent we were
coming through on the hondas me and
johnny on my fifty and wendel on his
and there in the middle of the yokum dorm

parking lot sitting all by itself at the
center of the perfect white plain was a
little honda a lot like ours and we
scooted and slid into the arena and parked

there by the third bike which turned out
to be a sixty-five barely bigger than ours still
we envied it it was like all i needed for
the world to be perfect was for me to have

that sixty-five and johnny on my fifty
and we sat there for a little smoking
looking at the ignition and wendel said do
you think we can hotwire it? and i just

reached under the seat because i knew
where to look on hondas and pulled the latch
and lifted it up to reveal the toolkit nestled
there between tank and fender and i took

it out and closed the seat and unrolled the gray
plastic pouch and took out the pliers
and with them loosened the bolt that held
the cowl around the ignition and when

i took that off got the philips screw-
driver and took off the two screws that held
the key switch to the frame and we
looked at it carefully there were four wires

feeding into the back of the thing and we
were saying stuff like white's always the
ground and black must be the hot but
what are the red and the green and in the

end i took my pocket knife and cut them all
stripped them and twisted them all four
together got on it kicked once and it started
and the three of us spun out of the lot sideways

rooster tails behind us sliding left and
right on the snow we rode up on markham
hill because we knew a shed up there that
nobody ever came to it was

covered in honeysuckle ground
to rusted-out peak of its
tin roof and we
jacked the hasp

off the door and stashed
the sixty-five inside it and we said ok we'll
leave it there six months and then every-
one will have forgotten about it

but of course next day we woke up and just
had to meet back at that shed and look at it
and then had to start it up just to see
and then wendel just said come on and we

took off down the hill and when we got
to the practice field on razorback road wendel took
off straight across it gunning for the slope
on the other side hit the peak at about

thirty and flew i swear to god ten feet
in the air i spun in behind him got it in
third by the time i crossed the field then
hit the jump pulling up on the front too

late came down far forward and went over
the bars face first sliding snow going down
my shirt into my mouth got up laughing then
johnny came up barely popped

a wheelie and we were laughing and pumped
went back down for another go when a
pickup pulls up on the street and these two
guys come running for us yelling you mother

fuckers we're gonna get you and i see them and
drop the sixty five on its side in the snow
and run to jump on back with wendel but
he sees them too and guns it and leaves me

jogging up the slope with the guys gaining
on me but then he stops at the top and waits
and i jump on and we take off down razorback
and i'm saying what the fuck

were you doing? and he said if i
stopped on that
hill i'd never get started again
and as we were getting away

i looked back and saw the guys
had stopped over the sixty-five still steaming
in the snow and they were looking at us
and looking back down at the bike

they didn't know it was stolen
they were just coming to kick us off the practice
field and later that evening we sat and
smoked and said jesus we were so dumb but

imagine what those guys thought did you
see them standing there with their
mouths open and we laughed anything
that made them feel like the idiots they were

pleased us immensely the slightest look of
befuddlement or incredulity was a great prize
once riding along we saw some kids
playing basketball in a driveway and we

rode right up under the basket
and wendel grabbed the ball and threw
it to johnny who was on back with me
and we rode off with it the kids' mouths

open their eyes bugging out i don't
know like you said how we didn't get killed
we'd fall get up wipe the gravel out of
the knee wounds

and get back on because nothing mattered
but the continuation at all cost
complete the circuit ceaseless
effort from the moment of waking to the brink

of sleep we hadn't
a minute to spare everyone
always said it was so totally safe
around fayetteville you could leave your house

open your keys in your car so really the
only thing holding us back was our own
sensitive conscience the firm conviction
yet also the desire also the necessity that

we be the evil and they be the good
and sure we'd mope around in guilt sometimes
but in truth never the slightest
temptation to switch sides what was there

after all in the good to tempt us?
what manicured lawns what star-
patterned formica what turquoise
appliance would ever cause us to consider

giving up the superhuman delight of being
the worst in school? the in-
corrigible the unrepentant the lost
the ones who didn't care because there wasn't

anything the adult world could do to them
and the other day
i was talking to a guy i know a poet
his name is christian and he was saying

how he just missed
how science is about to conquer death but it
will come just a little too late for him if only
he'd been born one generation later

then he would have lived forever
and i thought it strange that anyone
could believe such a thing
but it made me think what would it be like

to keep on living and living
like if i lived for two thousand years would
jimmy ball still be out at the end
of the driveway leaning against the maple tree?

and the preacher with cerebral palsy
at his pulpit for all those eons? and
wendel on his honda cigarette
dangling till the end of days?

caroline in the woods?
me and pop carrying the boards with the graffiti
on them? or would it be like the antennae
tower i used to climb it up

the side of the house you could go all the way to the
roof if you wanted and one day
i was sitting around not
doing anything and sort of

out of the blue said
to pop did i climb the antennae
tower and fall off it? asked this even
though i didn't remember such a thing

it just occurred to me for no reason
that it might have happened and
i didn't remember and pop said
yeah it almost killed you

and we never said another word about it
would it be like that?
would there be all
these immortal people

who couldn't remember having begun?
or would those be the chosen
of the earth the seers those
we lock in the memory wing

far from our own prying
eyes and momma says momma!
her eyes come open and
look at me and she

says it again momma! don't! looking
worried and then confused and then
i see myself coming into focus in her
eyes the look changing from urgency to

disappointment she lays back on the
pillow looks up at the
ceiling acoustic
grid meeting the gloss-

painted walls and
i say well i guess
i better go it's getting
dark and the snow's still falling

yes she says the roads and i say don't
worry i can drive it i'm pretty good in
snow i learned that year in van-
couver and she says it'll be bad tomorrow

and i say i'll be back
in the morning it doesn't matter
if the snow sticks
on the roads tonight

i'll put on the chains
if i have to don't worry
i can go most
anywhere in chains

PART II

To my father in the underworld

there was an order to it yes
things caused other things a progress
in time one-directional a one-way street
like the one you my father turned us down

the wrong way that time and a guy
walking along yelled one-way street mac
and you yelled back we're only going
one way i was embarrassed as usual

and playing catch in the back yard that day i hit
the limb overhead and showered you with stinging ants
can you put another log on the fire?
just while we're here talking?

it's funny i just had the feeling i
was never going to say that word log
again i don't know why i should
have that feeling i guess it makes

sense there has to be a last
instance of everything a last time i'll
say dog or goal or god or electricity a
last time i'll use words at all

can you stoke it a little? my hands are cold
and my feet are freezing it's dark as
thursday and i can't seem to get warm that's
a problem i've always had bad circulation

nothing really changes i guess even here
with you dead a dozen years now
and us still fucking
around with language don't you

find that a little surprising?
i heard the native americans called
writing dead bugs on bark
now we're dead bugs on bark

once in seventy and i don't know why
i think of this now but we all me and michael
and the rest went out to wedington found
a little clearing in the woods it was

richard who'd ferried us and we fell out
of his mustang into the lovely long green
hair of the grass already tripping
rolling in it petting it rubbing

our faces in it absorbing
the green and lazy wavy motion of it
and from above the dead or certain of the dead
looked down on us impassively they were

coursing this way and that in layers
wispy white death's-heads rib cages spindly
femurs radii ulnas indiscreet bodyparts
comingling coursing across the blue

blue sky stroked with bright outlines of
green and red which over time time that
might have been minutes or eons came
to surround encase and entangle the

bone-parts and the ghastly
heads responded open-mouthed
astonished white
translucent faces imploring

us to release them from the knotting of
the neon thread binding tighter and closer
until the entire sky was a mass of churning
van gogh color and the dead caught up in it

like a shipwrecked horde tossed in hull-
boards in crosses and sail-tatters in wave
upon wave of alphabets
bone-mash turning in letter-mulch

writhing in sea-writing
a sky-writing
white letters
en masse

and in the mass no single instance
or word to divert attention
not the least momentary distraction from
the ceaseless effort of turning things into

images and images into other things the all
being only the current the continuous circuit
of transmogrification till by and by there interposed a
shadow

dark and hooded
and the faces of the impotent dead flattened
and the harpy-haunted suicides
open their mouths in agony

as the three-headed one approached
flanked by homunculi and broken
crosses sullen marching giants
muscled and booted like workers

bearing the litter of the bird-headed
god of the vacuum
the god
who erases all

even the words
carved in the bone even the very
record of the dead and the feathered owl-
face of that god looked down at us

so it was that evening fell funny
how we always saw the same things
on acid as if they were indeed in the
world it was just that straight

people couldn't see them
nights we were hanging in the bars
that had started when i was nineteen
but on twenty-first birthdays

all the clubs on dickson street would give
a free beer so i went up and down the
street that night and at george's mary the
owner looked at my driver's license

looked at it and laughed because i'd been
in there every week for two years
and she gave me my free beer anyway
that was how great george's was

black and red on the inside low
cciling booths and tables
with goatteed beatniks
talking poetry art philosophy

little rooms in the back with
couches and signs that said couples only
but no one could even see the signs
friday nights it was so crowded

once i was playing chess with jim calhoun
and it gradually filled up around us filled
and got louder and louder with the juke
box cranked all the way and everyone

drunk and yelling teetering falling all
over us and we were fending the game from
falling bottles and bodies till it was like
that kley drawing staying power at cards

and all the while never breaking con-
centration and people would come and
stare in disbelief
but in the end a little

crowd formed around us to watch
the endgame and i was scared because
i was never that good at the endgame
i mean if i don't have my queen or at

least a rook i freak out at the
tediousness of it moving all those pawns
around one move at a time and you
have to count so meticulously but on

this night i was right there and i
got him and when he realized i was
going to promote and he couldn't stop
it he took his king and laid it on its

side a bunch of them cheered and i
looked up for the first time and they were
patting me on the back and buying me
beers and someone handed me a pitcher and

i leaned back and drank half of it straight
from the horn and brazier was there that night
and i was surprised he was watching the game
but he shook my hand and said all right

and then he leaned back against the juke
box and said this is the only place in the
bar where the music is loud enough he was
playing the rolling stones which was what

he always played and i asked if he'd
ever seen them and he said yeah i
caught them in new orleans a year
ago and i asked what it was like and he

said well we came into the hall and the
lights were up and the stage lights dim but
still you could see the wall of speakers up
there and you could tell the drum kit

was there just under a tarp and there was
a grand piano on one end of the stage and
these two guys were fucking around
running cables and duct-taping them to the

floor and then this guy came out and plugged
in a guitar and for a minute i thought it was
keith but when he started tuning it i said
that ain't keith but it sure as fuck is keith's

guitar and just this little taste of it has me so
worked up i just have to fight my way to the
front and i'm draggin peacock
with me even though she's saying jesus

twenty feet away is ok we're too close it'll be too
loud and i tell her there is no such
thing as too loud and we get right to the
stage where we can like lean our elbows

on it and i can see the guitar guy real
good now and i'm trying to figure out what
the first song is gonna be by the way he
tunes the guitar because keith you know is

famous for using a different tuning on
every song but i gave up on that pretty
quick because i don't know fuck all about
how to tune a guitar but anyway the

guitar guy and the cable guys finally leave
and they pull the tarp off the drums and they
put a glass of whiskey on the piano
and just walk off and leave the stage totally

empty and the lights are still low so it takes
the crowd a few minutes to notice but then
they take the house lights down just a little
and the crowd gets quiet like it is a single

animal and it has pricked up its ears
and every once in a while someone will
yell some random thing like just letting off
steam but mostly it is pretty quiet until

the chant starts up of its own accord jagger
jagger they're chanting in unison and it gets
louder and louder until it kind of starts to
peak and just when it peaks it falls apart

into pure noise and everyone is just screaming
and yelling and whistling and pleading and
swooning and i realized what i was seeing
a microcosm i mean the cave itself there all of us

writhing like worms in a darkened room
and i understood for the first time how
dante could see what he saw and live to tell
and smoke was rising up and it was getting

close and hot and i actually started to
get a little scared felt the crush and smell
of the crowd drug-crazed ecstatic panicking
there was no place to run in case of emerg-

ency we were in this to stay it was as i said
the world itself and how does one escape
the world? and then i heard even in that
din i swear i heard it a switch being

thrown it was a click just like a regular
light switch but louder and one lone
spotlight came on on the stage right
over jagger's mic stand and the crowd

hushed just like that just like that switch
that turned on the spot turned off
the crowd and we were all watching
that mic stand in silence holding our

breath what an
incredible thing a mic stand is
the sort of cross shape it has with its
omphallos at the top and the cable running

like an umbilicus into the electric heart of the
world and it was like i could feel the electricity
pulsing through that cable the
electricity the sound the vibration

like all these things were a single
sensation synaesthesia a single energy and that
energy was powering us all like
one heart was pumping through all our

veins i swear we beat in unison and i thought
i saw something moving in the shadows
in the back ghosts they were man-shapes
silhouettes shifting in the dark and

one walked out jagger
walking into the light and the crowd
started to yell again and the stage lights
came up and there was the band

and they made a few little scratchy
noises on the guitars and i understood
i think exactly what it
means to represent felt it you know

what a symbol is what mankind is
everything that blake was talkin about
and brazier stopped and took a swig of
beer and that he said was before

they ever played a fucking chord
and i looked at him for a minute and then
said yeah i'd like to see them some time
and he nodded and i said

you know as far as i'm concerned you could
ball up the whole fucking mass of english and
american and even world literature and throw
it in the trash but just keep one thing just

one little play and that play is in the jungle of
cities just keep that one brecht play and that
would be all and he looked at me a
little sideways or even shocked but then he

started nodding and said yeah you know what
lavender you're alright and after that we
were friends me and him and pea-
cock he called her peacock because

brecht always called his wife by her last
name i met up with them in canada
for a while after fayetteville me just fucking
around and them up there for philosophical

reasons not to escape the draft but to
be in a place where some semblance of
socialism was in practice we thought
it was pretty bleak back then and it

was this was just after my lai just
after calley was pardoned nixon
was about to go down and reagan
coming in and we shifted our stance

from knee-jerk socialism to radical communism
to an existential nihilism drawing
comfort and license from the lack
of hope it was this philosophy that

spawned many an evening at georges
or later back at someone's apartment
boyd and dave's place on fallin street listening
to velvet underground and slamming

around till the wee hours sometimes we'd
take the bikes out into the country
maybe ten of us on six or seven bikes
i had a three-o-five scrambler then best

bike i ever had and we'd ride out
one-o-one toward tontitown after
midnight and ride right into the vineyards
between the rows and lay out under

the stars and smoke joints and eat
muscadines squeezing out the sweet
fruit the juice running down our
arms and heading back from there one

night hit a curve at the bottom
of a steep drop and gravel on the road
and gilbert slid into the ditch he managed
to keep control and hopped out the

other side into the front yard of a farm
house before he slid down safely in the
grass the rest of us turned around and
joined him in the yard six

noisy bikes roaring around at two
in the morning everyone drunk and
yelling and we could see the farmer's
face in the window we finally got

gilbert back on his bike too
shaken to drive he rode on the
back and let someone else drive it
gilbert never was too good on that little

suzuki like one afternoon
we were out riding me and him and mike
and we came down a side road to a stop
sign at the highway mike and i in front

we stopped but for some reason gilbert
kept going ran smack into the side
of a car going sixty missed his maker by
a fraction of a second the car knocked

the bike out from under him sent it
spinning off down the highway and
he went up in the air spun around
a couple of times and landed on his feet

the car veered and spun out and hit
a post and the bike was all but trashed
but gilbert himself didn't even scratch
a knee he was a local and a little less

white-trash than the rest of us his dad
wrote for the paper and got every record
that elektra put out for free so we always had
the latest doors and it was over at his

house where i first heard the stooges
but after sophomore year gilbert discovered
real drugs hooked up with a red-headed
girl name joni twenty years his senior

and every once in a while we'd read
about a drug store burglary and then
there would be a party at their place that
would last six or seven days things going

downhill for a lot of people then
they would gather over there or over at
parker's and shoot dope till it ran out
preludin cocaine morphine dilaudid

they'd huddle over a stove for hours
cooking down filtering through a cotton
ball into an eyedropper with a plastic
grape for a squeezer then they'd hold it

up to the light flick it with a finger to
shake out the bubbles tying off belt in
mouth poking drawing blood then
squeezing the grape eyes half closed

we never shot up us we were acid
heads but hung out at the houses because
that's where the politicos hung and
where we bought our acid and weed

but then one time dave and i
picked up michael at a hotel room on college
and he came out smacking his
lips and all fidgety and we knew he was

speeding we didn't say a word
waited while he got in the back seat
and then sat there with his knee
jumpin up and down smoking and

grinding his teeth until he finally
yelled out yeah yeah yeah i shot up ok i
shot some speed do you hate me? yall
don't hate me do you? and we said nah

of course not and we didn't it was just
that he would even have to say it
that said it all and it was about this time
boyd moved back to town to go to

school and he and dave rented the house
on lafayette and we all read fear and
loathing in las vegas and tried to live
it there boyd eventually burned that house down

with the solvents in his painting room
in the back but while it lasted it was great
i left my guitar and amp there but
there were never enough instruments so

one night drunk as usual we rode the
bikes over to the high school and broke
into the band room made three trips
and then we had two drum kits and

saxophones a trumpet clarinet flute all
that eventually got pawned because no
one could play them and after boyd
burned down the house those that were

left were covered with soot just like
they'd been painted black boyd and dave
moved into the other half of martha and
doug's double on fallin street then

and that particular era ended in chaos with
dave getting busted for a pound of weed
and boyd going back to suburban life in
little rock it took us a while to figure out

that boyd had ratted dave out that was how
dumb we were i was the only one who
finished school very strange to reflect now
how much i read during that time i remember

as one long acid trip like in freshman
english i read the sound and the fury
the resurrection the field of vision the
crying of lot forty nine and nine other novels

plus in english survey stuff like bede
beowolf sir gawain and the green knight
chaucer twa corbies and westron wind
the cuckoo song piers plowman the

mystery plays morte d'arthur everyman
skelton more's utopia wyatt hooker
hoby golding edmund spenser sir
walter raleigh lyly and sir philip

sidney southwell drayton marlowe
shakespeare campion nashe donne ben
jonson bacon hobbes herbert vaughan
herrick suckling lovelace cowley

marvell milton dryden pepys bunyan
locke newton butler aphra behn
congreve defoe swift addison and
steele pope samuel johnson boswell

gray smart goldsmith cowper sir
patrick spens and lord randall and in
the second semester blake burnes
wollstonecraft wordsworth keats and

shelley coleridge sir walter scott hazlitt
thomas moore de quincey byron landon
carlyle newman mill both brownings
tennyson dickens fitzgerald's rubaiyat

bronte ruskin george eliot matthew
arnold huxley the rossettis swinburne
pater hopkins lewis carroll wilde shaw
kipling dowson hardy conrad housman

rupert brooke sassoon wilfred owen
yeats virginia woolf joyce's stories
lawrence eliot mansfield macdiarmid
robert graves george orwell beckett

auden dylan thomas henry reed edith
sitwell philip larkin doris lessing thom
gunn and at the same time in american
survey reading john smith and bradford

and roger williams anne bradstreet
edward taylor mather byrd jonathan
edwards franklin crèvecoeur john
adams thomases paine and jefferson

freneau irving cooper bryant emerson
hawthorne longfellow whittier poe
lincoln fuller harriet beecher stowe
jacobs thoreau frederick douglass

whitman melville's moby dick and
bartleby emily dickinson mark twain
henry adams booker t. washington
henry james jewett gilman wharton

dreiser crane london masters robinson
cather lowell stein frost sherwood
anderson sandburg stevens williams
pound h.d. eliot again oneill porter

millay marianne moore e.e. cummings
fitzgerald dos passos faulkner hart crane
hemingway thomas wolfe langston hughes
steinbeck penn warren roethke welty olson

bishop tennessee williams cheever hayden
jarrell berryman ellison bellow arthur
miller lowell gwendolyn brooks kerouac
and in the contemporary drama class

i read most of brecht beckett artaud
ionesco pinter ghelderode pirandello
shaw arabel sartre genet etc. and then just on
my own sitting in the library between

classes ulysses and beckett's novels ken kesey and
tom wolfe camus tom stoppard bergson
homer and catullus villon enzensberger
hesse and castaneda michel butor

baudelaire rimbaud apollonaire reverdy guillevic
michaux cendrars neruda vallejo parra lorca
jimenez kafka and of course the beats burroughs
ginsberg ferlinghetti kerouac corso levertov lovely

richard brautigan and john lennon's poems
and that's just what i can re-
member off the top of my head and
what i considered important doesn't

count the tons of contemporary iowa-
school garbage i devoured like it
mattered and of course god
knows what spiralled off into psyche-

delic lethe like mr. jones oh yeah
i forgot to mention fielding
all kinds of
foibles resulted for

example the aforementioned calhoun
whom i trounced in chess was
a pal of the barefoot skinny long stringy hair
type and somewhere in there he moved

in with a girl from fort smith named
cynthia what was her last name i can't
believe it but i seem to have forgotten
anyway i used to see her a lot as we hung

in the same english major hippie crowds
and she would get drunk or high and
was a big flirt sometimes even doing stuff
like following me into the bathroom and

grabbing my dick while i was trying to
pee and this sort of shenanigans gradually
escalated until once calhoun was out of town
and she called me up and said lets get

together and we went out to the bar
and she was saying i don't know i don't
really want to go back to the house you
know in his own bed and everything but

in the end that's exactly where we went
and started fucking pretty regular there-
after marx that was her last name cynthia
marx and i believe it lasted several

months until one night she called me and
said lets meet and i rode the three o five
down onto the campus in front of old
maine and she walked up there and

we sat under the big oaks as she told me
she was feeling constricted and wanted to
be able to hang out with her other friends
and at first i was just saying oh sure no

problem but then it was like some light
bulb of adulthood went off in my head and
i say oh you mean and fuck them? and she said well
yeah and i said oh and then i got on the bike

and drove down dickson street to dickson street
liquor went in and stuffed a pint of jim beam
down my pants then rode over to michael's
and drank it every drop everyone just shook

their head at my plight but of course i
was the only one surprised i guess i
had it coming and i held it against cynthia
for a while but she would come

back into my life a little later under a
strange circumstance and i'm going to
walk around as i talk its so cold in here
is that fire ever going to warm up the

room? the poets were
an interesting crowd
there was like i said brazier and then gary
ligi what clear and brilliant minds those two

had that came seemingly to naught and there
was ralph adamo and carolyn later to be c.d.
wright and biguenet whom we called big
net and crazy john stoss whom i saw get

up on stage with r.d. rucker at
a rally against the war where we
hippies were chanting peace now peace
now and r.d. got up and took the mic and said look

i'm gonna tell you how you find peace
you're gonna find peace by picking up the gun
you ain't gonna find no peace till you learn
how to shoot and defend yourself from the

man and stoss got up lumbering three hundred
pound white guy and said it's time we put our
guts on the line we've gotta stay here until
we're arrested no backing down let's tell them

and lots of people raised their fists though there
were lots also who just kind of looked around and
thirty minutes later it all dispersed nothing irritated
you more though than a bunch of hippies yelling

peace like that time i was marching and saw you
on the sidewalk caught your eye and you waved
me over but i pretended not to see we were
chanting peace now and later you said

it reminded you of nazi germany the way everyone
was chanting and you said the rhythm without the
words chanted hey hey hey hey hey hey and i thought
it was strange like you hadn't heard what we were

saying only the rhythm of it as if we'd been
speaking german or something and for just a second
there i saw it as you did the indistinct mass of derelict
humanity fists raised chanting idolatry in babel

and there was me among them like a
foreigner in your own house an alien from
your loins and i felt your paranoid tomcat
discomfort when i was in the room felt it

in the brain's marrow beyond articulation
seething in it four decades
the rage sustained me wishing you dead
seems petty now that you are of course but

then so does everything else so here
one more time for the eons let me say
again fuck off there's
no peace now as there was no peace then

liars and torturers at the head of our
table now as then nixon to the tiger cages
we used to shout he pardoned calley who
machine-gunned an entire village of women

and children when his soldiers had to turn away
sickened now as then the waterboarding father-
führer phallic ambrosial in a way your petty
racism your idiotic theories about negroid

intelligence seem quaint compared
to what's going on on earth today you would have
bristled at the idea of a black president but now
as then anyone can fill the role anyone can be

king for a day torturer for a day black white
man woman now as then someone will come to
lead the slaughter someone will puff themselves
up with a noble cause and high sentence a syntax

that is in the end only a chant only the dumb
thrumming beat of bootheels marching now
as then when leroy baugus who'd enlisted right
out of high school and came back almost immediately

in a wheelchair then let his hair grow and carried
a sign that said thank you richard nixon and we
on the hill above the stadium with our crosses
that spelled my lai when nixon's helipcopter passed

right over us and the crowd growled like
an animal the father führer now as
then when cynthia marx told me about the
night her father died how he came to her door in

his underwear and she knew he was dying and
went back to bed thinking thank you god
i fucked her in that bed when her mother was
at work she didn't come of course she didn't

want to come what was exciting about it for
her was that she didn't come that she
held me inside her impassive watched as i
melted and completed the succession of beds that

needed to be stained we drove down to little rock
that day and stopped and swam at the lake
outside russellville we had a tube and floated
way out to the center beyond the reach of the

families on the beach and took off our suits
rubbing bodies budding in the amniotic water
where our politics dissolved still too shy to even
touch her asshole i would imagine its texture

on my tongue as i came inside her imagining
that the day would come a succession of intimacies
leading to some further intimacy yet knowing
then as now that the succession was circular

continuous and thinking that was my exist-
ential discovery not knowing as i do now that
there is an end that the chain of reasons
has an end and that end is absence

nonentity nothingness in the summer of
seventy-one dave said he could get us jobs at
yellowstone so i said great and filled out the form
but instead they gave us jobs at fort courage arizona

it was the original set from f-troop they
moved it to a rest stop on the i-forty
just across the line from gallup
we drove

out there in my ford
wondering what we'd gotten into
we stayed in the barracks of the fort
and walked across the yard every morning to

work in the restaurant like the soldiers used
to pretend to do and there were two honda trail
nineties tied up outside that we could use
whenever we wanted and every day or two hippies

would pass through on their way to california
and we'd cop acid from them and drop and ride
out into the desert ride the trails until
we got lost nothing between us and

the stars we were reading castoneda but that really
didn't make any difference just being there
was the thing and the guy who
ran the place was one of those desert nuts he

caught us smoking a joint on the roof once and
took us down to his office sat us down paced a-
round back and forth couldn't decide what to
do with us he finally decided that we should write

confessions and sign them and he would keep them
so that if we fucked up any more that summer he
could send them to our parents and our school and
the fayetteville police and the arkansas state police

and he might even have to notify all the state police
between here and there new mexico oklahoma texas
arizona he didn't have to worry about because
the state troopers for that corner of the state

lived at fort courage there were two of
them cordoba and ryan cordoba was roving so
when he was in he bunked with us in the
barracks sometimes he would come in with

evidence bags of hash and sit down and smoke
it with us and us scared shitless lest we make a wrong
move once he took us for a ride in his patrol
car a hundred and twenty down the freeway lights

flashing siren wailing passing the hash pipe back
and forth ryan was a different story he lived
behind the fort in a trailer with his wife he
liked to sit on the overpass with his radar

and bust everyone as they came over the rise
and he would harrass the hippie hitchhikers and
search them and we used to comb the grass down
on the ramp where they were likely to be stopped

and salvage the dope they'd dumped when he
drove up and ryan always watched us
we'd see his head follow us as we drove by
and one day i'm sitting in the restaurant on

break drinking coffee and smoking and
ryan's wife sits down in the booth across from me
saying hey how's it goin and fiddling with the salt
shaker and she looks out the window at

some navajo kids playing under one of those scrub
desert trees one in diapers and three or
four older one in little cowboy boots and ryan's
wife says to me look at them out there will you that's

what they do they play around under a
tree for while and then they die
it's all so stupid and she put her elbow
on the table and her chin in her hand and

lolled her head to one side and says so what
do you do around here after dark? and i said not
much there ain't really much to do and she
rolled her eyes back at me and said yeah i've

been looking around for something to do
and she looked me right in the eye
and i was scared shitless not because i
wasn't interested but because

i was but lucky thing
next day dave and i drove to
albequerque jethro tull and mott the
hoople were playing and we stayed in the park

which was nothing but a tent city for hippies
with open-air cassette stores which also
sold hash and whites and mescaline and
whatever and we got high and joined

the crowd at the arena gathered outside the
doors with everyone getting restless because they
were refusing to open the doors until fifteen
minutes before the show and some guy in the crowd

put a brick in my hand saying throw it when
you see the first one go but we decided to check
the back entrances while all this was
brewing and that worked great we walked

right in the side door for free great show
everyone barefoot and flipping peace
signs and the arena full of smoke like some
giant pleasure dome and mott

carried us away the crowd awash
in mescaline floating above itself in a
skein of smoke and light and beach balls
and big balloons drifted around

the room leaving long
trails behind them and they would go on stage
and the band would bat them back
some nights we would go and play

at a bar called charley and mary's right
on the arizona new mexico border on
sundays it was packed because in arizona bars
were closed on sundays and it would fill up with

navajos and cowboys and road trash
and we were there buying beer
one sunday and dave just went up and asked the
band if we could sit in and they said sure

they weren't really into it anyway and we
went up and played johnny b. goode or some such
with the drunks wheeling on the dance
floor and people puking in corners and

we had a great time until that day when
a navajo at the bar started talking to me
head nodding he mumbled on about this and
that and then his words seem to come into

focus for one moment when he said i just
wouldn't want to see you guys get hurt and
after that the room had a different look
i saw the drunken eyes tracking us

from under their hatbrims and
we never played there again
on our way back to arkansas we
found a classic longhorn skull in the desert

i tied it on the hood and drove all the way
with it up there as if to say look
where we've been in the
valley of the shadow

and when we got to fort smith we decided not
to go home just yet but go on to little rock for a
couple of days and get drunk with
our friends down there boyd was there

boyd who one time
took off from little rock
in his parents' blue v.w. bug
four of us in it to see

the faces in memphis and
halfway there it starts clunking and
losing power and we stop at a gas station and
the guy says dude that's a rod knockin'

and he sells us a can of s.t.p. saying that'll get
us into memphis but actually it barely gets us
onto the freeway and we have to leave it by the
roadside and hitchhike in and we manage to get

to the show and drop our mescaline
and after the show i left them
found someone from fayetteville
to take me home

and boyd hitchhiked
home that night and to work the next
morning never saw his parents
talked a friend into towing the hulk back into

town and told his parents it
happened on his way to work
little rock was right
for boyd

right for a person of
his particular pretensions
he had a sneering
disdain for hippies and everyone

who hadn't yet learned what little
rock had to teach
the utter absence
of nostalgia fayetteville taught us that

nothing portends nothing but there was a
sense of fallen splendor of terrible waste
beneath the hopelessness which made
fayetteville seem tragic while little rock was

simply pathetic and not many people made the
transition between them gracefully like michael's
family when they moved down went seriously
to shit his momma died then his little

brother then his little sister melinda whom
i knew in fayetteville when she was about twelve
and would come down to the basement and
bother us while we were listening to records

and now o.d.'d she'd been home only a few weeks
and no one knew who her friends were but they
put a notice in the paper and two motorcycle gangs
showed up at the funeral sixty harleys and everyone

in their colors and michael went over to them
and said look it's ok if you guys are here but just
hang back while we're having the family thing ok?
and they said ok and hung back meekly until

the graveside service was done but for boyd
the move from fayetteville to little rock was
perfectly natural because he was from the
beginning little rock not fayetteville

he had no past no weight of history
to burden him his mother threw pots and
his dad was an adjuster and he sculpted in iron like
david smith and threw paint onto canvas like

jackson pollock and he made lithographs at
the art center in macarthur park and he came
to fayetteville and tested out of biology by
sitting behind someone with big glasses

but in the end fayetteville
was too much for him
and he went home to graduate from little rock coin-
cidentally about the time yates

came in for his one semester visit yates kicked
half of the usuals out of the poetry workshop
including me he told me i had talent but wasn't
ready and he gave us a reading list without

an american on it people like krolow guillevic
supervielle rilke breton arp and the french
crowd of surrealists also parra lorca neruda vallejo
and a bunch of his canadian pals like michael

bullock and also philosophers nietzsche
bergson merleau-ponty and i would bring him
poems and he'd talk about sense of resolution
and such and about halfway through the

semester i ran into him drunk in george's and he said
i want you in the workshop you hear i want you
in the fucking workshop and you're gonna get a
fucking a you hear you just get in the class and

you're gonna get a fucking a and so i had to drop
shakespeare and get about eight signatures on the
punch cards but in the end they got me in it under-
grad though i was it's on my record fall of seventy-

two and yates got in all sorts of fights with the poets
who were there especially miller williams
and when it came time for brazier to take his comps
he got all belligerent and did things like give his

answers in french or respond to the sense of the
sentence when it was just a grammatical example
and miller williams called up yates and said well
your philosophy has finally born fruit john

brazier has just ruined his academic career and
yates said what philosophy? i guess i'm
kind of partial to nietzsche
and after that it was all-out war

between yates's camp and miller's camp
made so much noise the campus
newspaper did a story on it southern writing vs.
yates with his antinationalism

and brazier dropped out with one month left
just to make his point he told me he had better
things to do like drive a garbage truck or what
he really wanted to do was go to belfast and

shoot british and at the end of the year i
asked miller if i could come into the m.f.a.
program and he said bill if i was your age i'd
use this time for travel and i decided that's what i

would do no real plan just leaving sold my three-
o-five for a measly hundred and fifty and took off
in the buick michael came with me we slept the
first night on a picnic table outside denver

in missoula we ran out of
money and i got a job carpentering
we were building forms and pouring
concrete every day

the boss would throw a tantrum if you moved from
point to point at a walk you had to trot all the time
me and the other guys on the crew snorted
coke to keep up

michael never did find a job up there and one day i came home
and he was gone and all my cash with him
he left a note saying sorry he'd pay me back some-
how and a few of days later they laid me

off and i left the next morning early with old fifty-
five on the radio had no plan but to go elsewhere
seattle was too gray so i turned north and went
on into vancouver called somebody at u.b.c.

who gave me yates's address with no compunction
at all and sweating it all the way i drove out west
to his house and walked up and knocked on the door
a girl opened the door i said is this mike yates's house?

and she went down into the basement
and after a while yates
came up stumbling as if we'd woken him and
he sat down before he looked at me and then

said oh yeah hell yeah annie this is and i thought
for a minute he was going to lose it but he got it
right bill lavender he said and annie said hi again
and he put me outside in his camper and i slept

on the tiny bed for a few days in the cold then
one day he says ok let's see what we can do about
getting you into u.b.c. and he said i'm thinking you
can live on the american side where

you can work and commute to u.b.c. a couple nights
a week and he picked up the phone and
called bullock and mcquirter who
was the chair and he said yeah guys i'd take this

121

as a personal favor if you'd take a look at this
kid's work he'd be a real asset to the program
and like if you guys want to get published at sono
nis some time well why shouldn't one professional

writer do that sort of thing for another? so i put
together a handful of poems in a file folder and went
down to the campus bullock liked one of the poems
mcquirter said hmmm maybe you should apply

and i ended up living in blaine the border town
because that's where the most work was i was
framing houses most of the time and driving up
to vancouver at night brazier and peacock came

up shortly after me they came seriously though
with papers to immigrate and they got an apartment
in north van and we'd go out to the weird vancouver
pubs where the waiters walked around with trays

full of draughts and just put ten or twelve on your
table when you waved they were like a quarter each
and we'd swill them till we felt like dancing
and then go looking for a juke box and we were

so poor one night a table full of drunk canucks
were falling over themselves and kicked over
their grocery sack and a can of dinty moore
beef stew rolled under our table and peacock

snatched it up and put it in her purse and no
one was the wiser but a little later they started
putting their groceries out on the table and one
of them says what happend to the beef stew?

and then the waitress whom we'd barely noticed
pointed over at us and then walked over and
pulled the can out of peacock's purse and one of
the flannel guys came over and picked brazier

up by the hair peacock rolled up into a ball
under the table and i held my breath
they stomped around the table in their boots
saying make no mistake we're gonna kick your

asses and finally we just got up and meekly
slunk away and in the car brazier was next to
tears and he said jesus lavender do you realize
what this means it means that bertolt brecht

was wrong and he emphasized that last word
as if such a thing were unthinkable
but i said no it doesn't i mean we just went through
a scene from a brecht play didn't we?

i was living then in a bungalow on birch bay
with some california hippies who came north for winter
because of the cheap rent
and one day a young family moved in

a guy and his wife and daughter and and they started coming
around and i got to know them especially her
patty was her name and after a couple of week the
guy said he was going into the mountains for a while

and asked me to keep an eye on patty for him
she had me in bed within a couple of days
and one of the other girls in the cabins was friends
with the local bikers and

they started having parties there with the
girls dancing naked and once while i was fucking patty
someone just walked in and sat down on
the bed he sat there a minute then got up and

she wiggled out from under me and grabbed him
pulled him back to the bed taking out his
cock and guided him inside her while i
watched she used to visit me in dreams and

tell me about the dream the next day
one night i dreamed she was sitting in a
swamp stirring a big pot over an open fire
and she looked up at me and she was patty

but she was a hundred years old and the next
morning she and the daughter were
gone and i never saw them again
and i got the letter from u.b.c.

saying the committee was
impressed with this
poem and that but would like
to see another fifty

pages or so and that kind of quantity
was quite beyond me then and i called mcquirter
from a pay phone and he said yes maybe it would
best for you to use this time for travel and that night

i went over to brazier's and he'd gotten the exact
same letter and he said they all want you to
travel don't they lavender?
and yates called to say yeah i guess i was the kiss of

shit and we spent a few weeks just hanging until boyd
arrived he came up in the van with camille and now
he was listening to opera and not doing any drugs
and the three of us rented a big house in downtown

blaine around the corner from the biker bars
it was a great house but camille and i cringed each
time we saw each other and then one night we
went to a party there in town and we brought

a bottle of southern comfort and boyd and i
were drinking it on the porch and he got up and
went inside and i heard
screaming and went in to see a pile of bodies

boyd on the bottom kicking with his engineer
boots he shook them all off in a minute and
stumbled outside and to the car and he got in
sobbing and camille holding his head and me

driving they left a couple of days later and left
me with that big house and no friends nor even
now casual acquaintances in a very weird town
and so one day when the rent was coming due

i packed up all my shit the albums and crappy
stereo and the guild guitar you bought me for
high school graduation and the smith-corona
electric typewriter and maybe thirty pages of

poems and radio plays and threw them in the trunk and
my clothes in the back seat and drove up to
vancouver to say goodbye to brazier and
peacock at their little basement space with a

shared bath it was their third apartment in
six months and they were sitting there reading
they looked like twins both spikey haired
short and skinny they could wear the same

clothes and always dressed like urban artistes
so different from me in my jeans and flannel
and i said i was leaving and peacock started to
cry but squelched it and brazier just said yeah

i don't blame you and we went out and had a few
beers and talked and i decided i was going to
go to new orleans and brazier said yeah that is the
thing to do and he made me a list of places to go

molly's irish and the seven seas and billy's home
cooking and frankie and johnny's and he drew me
a map that showed canal and carrollton parallel and
saint charles running between them he'd never ever

seen a map of the city nor had he ever driven
a car then we went back to their place and sat
around for a while until brazier passed out and
i told peacock i guess i better go and she was shaking

him saying john come on bill's leaving you have to wake
up but he could not be roused and finally she gave
up and came over to give me a hug and i bent over
and she grabbed me with all four feet and kissed

me hard clutching sucking taking my breath away
and i dropped down on top of her on the couch
only because my knees gave way but she just
looked at me and said get out of here and i did

and never saw either of them again
i drove the northern route through
the dakotas gray blank skies and brown
rolling fields of wheat as far as i could see

broke down in kansas city but it was
just that the the points weren't breaking
got back on the road next morning and
pulled into fayetteville noon of third day

i didn't know what to do
drove around campus till i heard someone
yell my name and saw marvin on his porch on whitham
and got out and smoked a joint with him

and this girl walked by in a flannel
shirt and cutoffs and marvin said hey
debbie and i asked marvin
what everyone was up to and he said not much

most of the poets i knew had graduated he had
too actually and would be moving back to little
rock soon and i bummed around
couch to couch for a week before i came home

it was supper time and
i was hungry momma was
in the garden stooped over
and you were mincing

around with the hoe like you did
and i told you the story of the drive from seattle
complete with the car breaking down as if
it had happened just then and we ate in the kitchen

like normal and then i picked up the phone and
pretended to call someone and said i need to go
out can i borrow ten bucks? and you gave it to me
and i went back down to dickson street we'd drink

in the bars till they closed at midnight then we'd
go to one apartment complex or another and go
swimming and debbie was working at george's at
the time finishing up her b.a. and she

came swimming with us one night and dave and
i threw her in she took it pretty well dave and her
had had a thing for a while but one night he said
to me well debbie says that we're done because she's

interested in you so and he paused but not for very
long have fun and a couple of weeks later i woke
up in her bed with the phone ringing and her in
the bathroom and i answered it and the woman on

the other end said what? who is this? where's debbie?
and i went and got her and she hemmed and hawed
and later her dad called back and said jesus will you
answer your own fucking phone? and they cut her off

after that and i had to go to work to pay the rent on
her apartment i was framing houses in springdale
and going out every night and she would get mad
at me and throw things when i'd flirt in the bars

but we always made up and there was a new
batch of poets in town i was sitting in
on the workshop at miller's house
and we'd see frank stanford in the bars sometimes

and everyone would always say are you
writing anything? and most of us would say not
really but frank would always say yep i am
i'm at it we all knew he was the real poet

among us that this was his moment and the rest
of us were just waiting and carolyn took up with him
soon after that and even moved in
with him and ginny they were a three-

some for a while at varying levels of comfort
if rumor can be believed
i gave frank some poems once
and he looked at them and said

well
i was getting interested in a character here and then
the whole thing changed i look
at what's here and think of the future and i'm

not really sure what to expect and then years
later i happened to be back home at your place
and the phone rang and it was of all people
cynthia whom i hadn't heard from in years

she still had your number from the old days
she said frank stanford shot himself last night
i said no kidding and she said
yeah and they were both there ginny and carolyn

so what happened? i said
and she said i don't know but i just have to think
and i got off the phone and you
and momma looking at me

and i said to deb that was
of all people cynthia
she said frank stanford shot
himself last night and deb went oh

and you said a friend of yours? and there was
then as now
no way to describe what he was to me
and there still isn't

momma used to say be careful what you wish for
you might get it she wouldn't dare think
you always get what you wish for
be careful what you wish for you always

get it the world is
reflection of our desire
like that summer i was
looking for a car and

saw an old pickup with a for sale sign
we were down near mount gaylor for some
reason and saw this cherry black fifty-one
ford in the front yard of a farm house and

stopped and talked to the guy and all he wanted
was two fifty for it it was absolutely perfect not even
a rip in the seat the engine had been rebuilt even
repainted it started on first crank and i saw

myself in it cruising dickson street like some
arkansas low rider and i could put the bike in
the bed if i needed or help people move or take
the gang to the lake or do just anything you can

do with a pickup the bench seat was great for making
out and all around it was to be the best possession i'd
ever had and i only had about fifty bucks in the
bank but i bartered with the old guy and wouldn't

let it go and he finally agreed to take weekly
payments till i paid it off and i gave him thirty
right there and then sent him thirty each week
from my ralston purina turkey processing plant check

till finally after six long weeks i was ready to pay
it off and dave drove me out there with the last
twenty bucks in my hand and gave it to him
and he signed over the title and i drove it

back to town and parked it out front of
the duplex on watson where dave and i
were living at the time and then since i'd
gone straight out there from work i decided to

take a bath and i wanted to celebrate a little but
had only a couple of reds so i took those and
poured a glass of wine and sat in the bathtub list-
ening to music relaxing in the warm water

drifting off in a lazy jimi hendrix haze came
to underwater inhaling soap and water coughing and
flailing over the tub edge climbing out
shaking myself awake only the thought of the new

truck got me going and i got dressed
and went out to take her for a spin because
i knew if i sat around i'd pass out again and i drove
down dickson watching the heads turn

then on up toward campus
turned in front of the old engineering building
where they still had angle parking in front and
even though it was six o'clock or so on a friday

there were a lot of summer students around boys and
pretty girls and i was watching their skirts
in the gentle june wind driving slow maybe twenty
but even twenty seems fast when you run into

a parked car which is what i did bumped
my head on the wheel jolted awake and looked
around now it was the pretty girls' turn to look
at me and they were i'd run into

the tailgate of another pickup and messed it
up pretty bad and my first thought was that i was
going to jail since i was way beyond pretending
to be sober so i cranked her back up and she cranked

just fine only now when she ran the fan clanged on
the radiator at every revolution so we made quite a
commotion driving across campus and every walking
student turned and looked at us and i got it down just

off campus on one of those little dirt lanes in
the hollow and left it there and walked to michael's
and he got me some coffee and slapped me around
a little and we came up with a plan to call a wrecker

and get the truck towed out before anyone was
the wiser and that's what we did and i rode with
the wrecker driver to the station and thought
everything was going to work out until i saw the

cop standing there as we pulled up you labbinder?
he said as i got out and i said yeah and he said you're
gonna have to go talk to university police about the
vehicle you damaged and i said ok sure that would be

no problem and secretly i was just thanking my lucky
stars he hadn't noticed how fucked up i was and then
he said you know what i wouldn't drive any more till
you sober up and i said ok and went to see the u. of a.

cops they gave me a name and address and said this
is the guy whose truck you smashed and he is some
pissed his name was geist he was a janitor at
the old engineering building i knew the geists

they were a white trash family i'd known in grade
school there were two of them in my grade arthur
and frances and they came to school dirty and
stinking and we would make faces and go gross if

one of them touched us and i remember once in
fifth grade when arthur was called on
in spelling bee the teacher actually gave him the word
cat and he put his finger to his chin and said

questioningly w r r?
i went to the engineering building on monday
to see arthur's dad and he
stomped around talking about

how hard it was to make it on
what he took home and now
some drunk student has to go and mess up his
truck hit it so hard he had to replace the battery

the fucking battery he said the blow knocked
the fucking battery off the mount and cracked it
so that was almost twenty five bucks right there and
then he was going to need a new tailgate and some

body work so it would latch it was liable to
be three hundred bucks before it was done and where
was he supposed to get that kind of money? and he
looked at me then and said what was you drivin any-

way? and i told him about the fifty-one ford and he said
a fifty-one no shit? and he looked at me and sized
me up a bit and must've finally seen that i wasn't
a frat boy so he said all right then you bring me what

you can every week till you pay it off just bring it
to me right here in the engineering building every
friday when you get off and i said ok i'll do it
and he said you do that because if you miss

a friday i'm gonna walk straight down to the
police and tell them you're a deadbeat and to
go pick you up and i said ok don't worry i'll
bring you some money every friday

we were standing in the stairwell
on the landing between the
first and second floor and
from then on every

friday i came to the engineering build-
ing and found him on that landing looking
out the window at the frat boys and sorority girls
and hippies and r.o.t.c. geeks walking across the quad

i was taking home about sixty bucks a week
and would bring him twenty or thirty
the total damage being about a hundred and fifty and the first
couple of weeks i gave him the

cash and he just nodded and i said see you
next week but one friday when i handed him
the money he kept looking out the window
instead of taking it said where was it you said

you worked? and i said the turkey plant in
springdale and he said oh yeah that's right
and then he said i got kids your age did you
know that? and i said yeah i went to school

with them arthur and frances right? and he
turned and took the money from me and looked
at it and then he said
yep that's right arthur and frances

a couple of weeks after that when i brought
him the payment i said so just two payments
after this one right? and he said
no this one is it

this is your last payment
because i know how it is
and that was the last
i saw of the geist family

i did get the truck running again had the
radiator cored put it back in myself bending the
mounts back as best i could but
the fender was crushed down into the tire

and there was nothing i could do
but take it off and so i could still drive
the thing but now instead of a cherry old
truck it was a bent-up hulk

same truck different meaning and
in the end i gave it to pete and let him pay it
off the same way i had paid it off twice now
pete was a friend of me and mike and dave's

from high school but he shot a lot of dope hung
out with gilbert's crowd and he'd disappear
into one house or another with them when
they would tap a drugstore and i hadn't

seen him much that year but in the fall of
seventy-two i was taking a journalism class from
a teacher named calahan and some of the
kids in that class wrote for the campus paper

we would talk about the news every morning
in class especially if something big happened
and one morning something big had happened
a female student who lived down

on center street had been killed the night
before stabbed to death in her bed and calahan
decided to devote the class to this
kind of story like when you could

use the girl's name and what to do if a cop or some-
one gave you information but said don't
quote me and how you always had to get two
sources on shaky information and whether it

was okay to call the girl's parents and pump
them for details and how much investigation a
journalist might actually do himself and how
much you just let the cops do and how you could

get in trouble if you got in the cops' way and
also one student brought up how important
it was to respect the police and keep your contacts
in the department happy so they would call you

and not someone else when something
happened this kid worked the city police
for the campus paper and he'd gotten the call
at four thirty in the morning

and he'd gone down there and hung out with the cops
now the whole class was watching
and he leaned back crossed his legs and starting talking
about it like it was no big deal just the sort of thing his

contacts were always letting him in on and finally
someone says well did they catch the guy? and he
says oh yeah they got him and now everyone
is wanting to know who the killer

is is he a student? is he a local? and the
kid pulls out his little notebook and flips some
pages and says wallace peter kunkel
who happened to be my friend pete and the

room got quiet and for a second and i said
so is this guy a suspect or is he the guy? oh technically i
guess he is a suspect but they found him right out-
side and he had blood all over him so they are

fairly certain and he's obviously a drug
addict and that evening on the front page
of the paper and i mean the fayetteville paper not
the campus thing there was a picture of pete

being led into the station in handcuffs and momma
saw it and remembered him and said good lord
did he do it? and i said no he didn't do it and it's
horrible what they're doing to him but i was

also starting to wonder myself because i knew
what happened to them when they were running
preludin or cocaine and hadn't slept for four
days and really most anything could have been

possible and we went over to michael's and
none of us could find out anything
the kid in journalism had his contacts
but we couldn't find out shit and next morning

it was all over the front page of the paper again
they were talking about the drug
addict son of well-to-do parents who lived out
in rolling hills and there wasn't one of us

who had even met his parents and when we
called his house no one answered and they wouldn't
let him out on bail because they said he was a flight
risk and his parents hired a good local lawyer

niblock was his name he did some work for a.c.l.u.
and things like that and they had the arraignment
and the charges were filed and they still wouldn't
let him make bail and the trial was set to start in

a couple of months but after about two weeks the
story naturally went dormant and then one day
on page two there was half a column saying that
they had released him because the blood on his

coat did not match the victim's and when i went
to journalism class the next day they didn't even
bring it up and that night michael called me and
said he'd gotten a call from pete

we picked him up from his folks' house
and drove up on markham hill
we'd brought him a couple of joints which
was all we had and he lit one and took a long drag

and said shit man and we said what happened? and
he said he was just out walking that night and he'd
gotten a little sloppy with some demerol and there was
a drop of blood on his sleeve one fucking drop of blood

but they saw the tracks on his arm and that did it
and it took them all that time to get around to test-
ing the blood type legal fees for the whole thing ran
thirty grand and his parents had been getting all

kinds of hate mail and threatening phone calls
so they had decided it was ruined for them here
and they were moving back to wisconsin
and not only that they were moving

back tomorrow and then he said hey mike can
i pick up my albums from your house before
i go? and michael said yeah sure so we drove
over to his place and got the albums

and then i drove pete home and he said see you
later man and shook hands and he walked
up into the front porch light with blonde
on blonde under his arm and dylan's big

face looking out and i never saw him again
and never got up the guts to raise my hand
in journalism class and talk about what journalism
and the police had done to pete but toward the end

of the semester calahan asked everyone to schedule
a meeting with him so i did and went to his office
and sat down across the desk from him we talked
for a few minutes about assignments and whatever and

then he looked down and set his jaw and said bill
how interested are you in journalism? and i said well
i'm interested in changing it and he said changing?
and i said yeah like you remember the girl who got

murdered and the kid they arrested that innocent
guy they put all over the front page when he was
charged and forgot about when he was released?
well that guy was a friend of mine from high

school and calahan said well bill that wasn't
journalism's fault we have to report i'm sure
you understand and i told him i was sure i
understood too and then i left i think calahan

gave me a c not that it makes any difference
what's that? clearing your throat? now
that's a noise i haven't heard for a while
it used to drive me crazy that constant

ahemming through breakfast you called it
asthma but it was asbestosis and would
finally kill you about a million ahems later
but the funny thing is that here up here on

this ledge where we sit around our little
joke of a fire our fire that lights but does not
warm up here the only one making any noise
is me and sure enough that little cough came

out of my own throat i heard my
self and thought it was you i guess
i picked up that cough just like i picked
up so many turns of phrase from you at the

breakfast table the tobacco in my case having
done what the asbestos did to you well let's stoke
the fire since i'm freezing as usual and the smoke
doesn't seem to bother you now it feels like

we're sitting on an edge looking out doesn't it?
over a lake or some other expanse how
would it be to jump do you suppose? we used to
off a rocky point just like this one

on beaver lake there was a place we always went
because no one else went there it was called
pleasure heights on the map which was odd
because it was as unfriendly a lake access as you

could find rocky and steep but martha and doug
always brought their chaise lounges and set them
up on the rock and she would lay out in her
bikini oiled and tan with that peach fuzz

around her navel and we'd drink beer and get
high and dive off the rock and scramble back
up the bank sometimes there would be ten of us there
on a saturday afternoon two or three car

loads and me and michael on my three-o-five
and one day a hippy showed up that none of us
knew and we shared our dope with him and took
turns diving off the little rock but then he comes

climbing out dripping and sits beside me and
points across the lake it was only about a hundred
yards wide there at the high bluff on the other
side and he said i want to dive off that

and i said yeah we swim over and jump off
it sometimes no one's ever dived though it's
about forty feet and he said i want to dive it
someone had a little skiff that day and

we loaded it up with beer and some swimming
and some paddling we set out for the other side
two stayed in the boat below the bluff and the
rest of us swam down to a swale in the rock

that was climbable and then at the top we
each went to the edge and looked over and some
then elected to walk back down which was
way harder than climbing up because you couldn't

just jump you had to run and leap to get out
where the water was deep enough and we talked
about how you had to land straight and fold
your arms to protect your neck and the hippy

said no i'm going head first that's the best way
trust me i've done this a lot and i thought
about it because i had done it a good bit myself
but in the end i ran and jumped waved my

arms a bit to straighten up felt the fabulous
vertigo of free-fall and landed about as
close to perfect as i could have hoped
for and still came up feeling like i'd been

socked in the jaw then dave and mike and
some of the others jumped and we were hanging
on to the side of skiff watching from below and
the hippy comes to the edge and yells down

at us that he's going to dive now and we said
ok come on and he disappeared for a moment
then came flying out in a swan arms back back
arched nice form like you'd see on tv and

he drew his arms forward into position for
a splashless entry about ten feet too soon
and landed flat on his back
someone said that guy's dead

and we all watched the bubbles where he'd
gone in already starting to think what we
were going to do with this dead hippy that
none of us knew but after a few seconds his

head bobbed up and he just sat there treading
water and staring at us wide-eyed
we asked if he was ok but he didn't answer
just kept treading water so we took the skiff

over to him and he grabbed the gunnel and
managed with our help to get himself
in and he sat in the front while we took him
back across and then he sat down on the ground

and never said another word the entire day but
he would look at me now and then with a
look like he had something really important
to say but had forgotten what it was and his

lips would try to open but wouldn't and i
got the idea that language had been knocked
out of him all his alphabets dissembling and
scrambled in his head and we left him there

wordless on the bank i assume someone took
him back to town but who knows
who knows what happened to any of them
who had their alphabets knocked around

just after i had moved in
to deb's apartment
i needed an office chair to type in
so i went down to old maine

one summer evening when the campus was
empty and got one i was wheeling
it down the sidewalk when a campus
cop walked up and said what's going on

what's with the chair?
and i said i had found it up there on the side-
walk and assumed it had been thrown away
and he said oh yeah well ok let's go sit in my

car and just let me write this up and so we did
and he's writing stuff and radioing and i'm
asking what's going to happen you're not like
calling the city cops or anything are you? and

he said oh no it's just an on-campus report you
might get some kind of a ticket and no sooner
did the lying sack of shit say that than a city
car pulls up beside us and i get handed off to

them and dropped in the tank and with my
one phone call i had to call deb's feminist
professor friend where she was having dinner
and i said hey i'm sorry to spring this on you but

i'm in jail and i need someone to bring me
some money so i can make bail and she says
you're kidding right? and then she came down
and got me out the campus cops reported

that the chair was worth more than five
hundred dollars to make the charge a felony
and the cop at the counter told me that and
said yep son looks like you're in real trouble

and then he busted out laughing and walked
away they knew it would be thrown out but
while they had me wanted to have a little
fun the real effect of the thing though

came the next day when the police
report came out in the paper there was my
name and deb's address and her landlord saw it
picked up the phone and evicted her because

they didn't allow unwed couples so that led us
to rent another apartment together and we ended up
having our wedding party there so stealing
the office chair set me on the road to legit-

imacy while cussing out the good father had
no effect at all or at least none that was ap-
parent though perhaps like the butterfly wing
reverbrating down to this very conversation

as the stolen chair balanced with marriage
balancing now with this civility
this summary of summery equivalents
through over-

correction and adjustment like sitting on
the teeter totter when i was a kid my butt
on the ground and then you coming along and
sitting on the other end that was an

overcorrection and my marriage to deb would
be an occasion where the teeter totter dropped
that's for sure after the wedding at your
house we went home to the apartment on

watson and had the real party
maybe fifty people some of the poets like wes and
marvin were there and wes had a black eye
and i asked him where he got it and he just sort

of blushed and said yeah you know marriage
is great you get to know each other it's
really weird and we decided right after that we
were moving to new orleans i still actually had

that map brazier had drawn on the napkin in vancouver
but first we moved to little rock for the summer
deb's mom got me a job at the employment
security division so we could make some

money before arriving in new orleans with
nothing and no plan i worked in research and
statistics and travelled around the state with
a guy named nowak doing surveys of unem-

ployed people asking them if they wanted
vocational training and if they thought it would
help them i can't imagine a more morose
life than that of the travelling bureaucrat i was

just nowak's assistant so i rode with him and
stayed in his motels and got a glimpse of his
life of leisure suits and holiday inn bars and
conventions where everyone slept around

he boasted about his sexual exploits like a
teenage liar but i never really saw him get
lucky except one morning i knocked on his
motel door and i heard some shuffling around

and he opened the door just a crack and peeked
out and i said are we going in to the office? and he
said no we're gonna be late today give them a call
will you? and i said what's up? and he said oh i've

got some old girl in here and she's a little shy
and i listened and looked for any evidence that
he wasn't bullshitting me again and found none
so i went back to my room and called the local

office and told them we'd be a little late
and later i asked him who she was and
all he would say was some old girl
i was glad when they took me off the road

and put me in the basement downtown that
was where i first worked on a computer we
calculated the stats we'd gained from our
survey around the state by sorting i.b.m. punch

cards and then i would enter the data on a
terminal neon-green text on a black screen
i had a honda one seventy-five i drove back
and forth to work me and deb had rented

a one room studio in a sad little burb off
pine street and the guy who lived in the rest
of the house with his invalid mother
had installed an electric bell like a school bell

that his mother could ring if she needed something
while he was out in the yard or even down the
street and that bell would ring at all hours
and every time it did we thought the old lady

must be dying the place was so small we had
to move the coffee table to unfold the couch
to sleep on and the bed felt like a blanket
draped over two pipes and it killed my back

finally we moved out and into her folks'
basement which was way more comfortable
her mom was a statistician for the state
and al her dad was a furniture rep he travelled

all over the south selling office furniture
al was always good to me we would
sit outside and smoke and drink beer and
he would tell me stories about his life about

working for aramco in dhahran where deb was
born and coming back to the states with a pot-
full of money and then looking off into the yard
saying yeah but we blew it we sure did and

if i'd done it right fern wouldn't be working
for the state right now i'll tell you that and
i asked him what happened and he said well
we just got tired of it the desert and the lack

145

the lack of everything there were you know no
clothes to buy everything we had came from the
p.x. at the base i could have gone just a few more
years and had a good retirement but i had some

money saved and thought i could make something
happen back here and i don't even know how
or why we came to little rock but once i saw it
i loved it and went and talked to a couple of bankers

and one of them introduced me to the governor
and then i knew it was the place for me so i
rented a space a sizeable little space downtown six
thousand square feet and set up shop

we made high-end powder-coated signs
the finish on them was just like
on that car right there we formed them out of
sheet metal painted them and baked them

in thousand degree ovens they were beautiful
a lot of them are still out there i have to say you
won't find a sign made like ours were these days
and i asked what would one of those sell for and

he said oh we didn't sell them that wasn't the way
it worked what we would do is find a customer
who wanted to advertise let's say on the highway
between here and hot springs and we'd go out and

find a piece of land and we'd lease it you see
not a big plot just say ten feet square and we'd
just lease the right to put a sign on it for a hundred
years and then we'd put up a pole and we'd have

electricity run to it and put one of our signs on it
and the customer would pay us so much a month
it was a great business but the problem was it
required so much capital up front and after a while

we just had more paper floating than we could
borrow money on and besides that i had hired
a guy to handle the books and i looked one
day and we had receivables out the ass

and no leverage to collect them but
to threaten to take down the signs which in
itself was a fairly expensive operation and i was
an idiot of course because instead of shutting

down right then and focusing on managing the
existing leases i used the withholding to keep
the factory running another couple of months
before i finally had to shut it down goddam

you could have heard a pin drop in the place
saddest thing i ever saw then i.r.s. came in
and sold all the equipment sold the leases as
well i guess i don't even know though i still

see the signs all over and that was when fern
had to go get a job which was something she
never bargained for and i had of course to pay
off the withholding that stuff doesn't go away

in bankruptcy you know so i got a job at the
base in greenland because if you stay
out of the country for a whole year you don't
have to pay any taxes and i did that three years

and got out from under i.r.s. anyway so at least
fern could bring the china back from her
sister's house and he lit another cigarette
he chain smoked and always thought with

everyone else that it would one day kill
him but it didn't he died of leukemia
and when that summer started to wind down
we made a run to new orleans to find an apartment

we called ralph and told him
we were coming he said you can't stay here
but we did anyway he and martin his brother
had a top floor on marengo we slept in

the back room they had a party while we
were there stoss came and made fish-head
soup which was tolerable but for the scales
and we looked at apartment after apartment

and they all sucked and were too expensive
and we missed the one we wanted on prytania
by an hour and deb started hitting the dashboard
and crying in frustration and it sort of scared

me but then she just sat up and said ok forget
it don't worry about me let's go to the next one
and finally we found a place that was great on
carondelet down by jackson it was two hundred

a month which was more than double the most
we'd ever paid but we took it and went back to
little rock to pack up our shit and when we told
al and fern how much the apartment cost they

were shocked their house note was less than that
and as time approached we rented a u-haul and
a tow bar for the toyota and the day before we
were driving down loaded it up everything but

the bike because i felt like going for a ride i don't
know why and i shut up the truck and went inside
the house was quiet like houses get sometimes
but for the squeaking floorboards as i walked

around and it made me want to be quiet too
and i found deb downstairs in the chaise
lounge reading smoking her benson and hedges
and she looked up at me and said all set?

and i said yeah and she made a face like she
was getting ready to do something scary
i said i'm going for a ride i'll be back in
a little while she nodded and said i'll be here

i rode south down university
to where the town began to thin
i saw what looked like a failed sub-
division a cleared tract across a couple

of low hills with concrete streets and power
lines and street lights but no
houses the whole site covered
with tall grass and scrub and even

some small trees making a comeback and they
had dumped truckloads of dirt in the entrance
road to keep people out but i rode over them
easily the streets were cracked weeds

poking through here and there
and from the pattern of the streets
i could see the work as it had been planned
the bare outline of it like a drawing

and i imagined you there running the job
the concrete trucks and carpenters
the stud walls rising up
the pounding of the hammers the shrieking of the saws

but there was nothing in that waste-
land as if fire had swept it clean clean
as that promontory where you rest now
and i rode the broken streets

but after a while it began to feel point-
less out there by myself and i stopped in a
cul-de-sac and shut it off
lit a cigarette and sat there

out west i could see woods and farmland the
city had not yet claimed and north the city
proper the university and the mall and down
south there was a subdivision like this one

except constructed with its curving
streets lined with houses
clean lawns and fences and addresses
painted on the curbs and i looked down and

saw that the address was painted on the
curb at my feet and i imagined the surveyors'
marks lost out in the weeds
each unit conceptualized

each with a number before
it even had a place and i imagined all those
numbers in a book somewhere still waiting
for the names to be filled in

PART III

To my sons, from the underworld.

hello is
what i said
behind the surgical mask
i was still hanging over her though

there was no need her
ravaged body inert even her voice
her screams now drugged to a somnolent
whisper and the o.b. gave a little

tug on the cord plopped the blue mass
into a bucket at his feet and said
one perfectly healthy afterbirth shall we
name it? and i went over and looked at you

swaddled in your plastic tub and you
looked back saw yourself in my eyes for
the first time red bewildered face
head squashed elongated bruised

from the pincers they'd used to pluck you
out when her numbed body failed and i
nothing but a pair of green eyes between green
mask and green hat and i said it again hello

a slight rippling of the mask your first
word what mystery among so many
mysteries first sign within first mirror
years later you'd have your fear of

masks wouldn't go into a room if
there was a mask on the wall mardi
gras finally cured you of it but there was
a year when i'd lift you on my shoulders

hold you up to the float and you'd ask
to be put down not even the insatiable
desire for baubles could overcome that
proximity to the mask and then one day

the phobia was gone and now you don't
even remember it well i'll
be your memory let me be your
mammal memory it's all i'm

good for really there aint that
much to do here in
paradise
but sit around and call up

other peoples' memories
hijos mios
three years later in the same
hospital your brother

had a softer landing his
tempered by our experience
knowing now what to ask for
proper timing of the epidural etc.

lives marked divided into sections by
hospital visits so aren't these white
surfaces our real mother? what a comfort
to be wheeled again into it to relax

all control to give yourself up to its order
its bare walls and bright lights
its smell of alcohol its tanks and tubes
shining needles and electronic pulses

after you both had feet under you
and i was off in that world of symbols
world of men and women and money and
their exchange i sat one morning in the

cafeteria of a small hospital in new
orleans east having coffee with their con-
struction manager and my partner jimmy said
what can we do for you barry? and barry said

well we've got this new operating room in
orthopedics you know right there next door
to the one you renovated last year and they're
getting negative pressure for some fucking

reason and here with the room already
scheduled i've sort of got my dick in my hand
because corporate's coming down for a walk-through
day after tomorrow so what i'm wondering is

if there's any way you could send someone out
to take a look at it off the books
i know it's a big deal and all i can say is
i'll make it up to you down the road somehow

we've got three or four things coming out for
bid maybe i can get you a little sneak-
peak at the other bids or something
anyway you think you can help me out?

and jimmy says sure no problem we'll send
someone out this afternoon and later driving
back i say to him man you always give
in too easy these fuckers make

more money than god but everything they
want from us we gotta do for free you know
what he told me? he said the real break-even
point on that facility on that little chickenshit

clinic is twenty five percent occupancy
ten fucking beds pay for that whole twenty
million dollar facility and the rest is gravy but when
they want us to do something for them we have

to do it for free and jimmy says i know i know but
we gotta be there we gotta be the one they call
when they've got a problem and i say ok fine and that
afternoon we get a sub to send out an h.v.a.c. tech

and we send a carpenter to move ceiling
tiles and a few minutes after they get there we
get a call from the carpenter and he's freaking
out saying he aint coming back to this job ever

because he went down to o.r. and they put him
in scrubs and let him through with his ladder
but right there on the counter just out-
side the door in a plastic tub was

a dead baby they just left it there he said
while the nurses was doin something else
they just left it lie there i can't work around
that nobody could expect me to work

around something like that
and jimmy gets on the phone with him and
tries to downplay it tries to
talk him down like there was some-

thing that could be said that could
defuse a situation like that we did
a lot of work for doctors in those days a lot
of doctors and a lot of those sleazy little

worms like barry who hung around just to
set up deals and make a little on the skim
and working for them was bad enough but
even worse was the obligatory socializing like

when some corporate geek from humana would
come in from louisville and me and jimmy and
barry would take him out barhopping in
metairie because they always wanted to go to

metairie never the french quarter and get him
drunk and do some blow and basically do what-
ever we could to keep him from even visiting
the job site and next morning up again at five

thirty and out of the house at six before your
mother or you even woke up because that's
the first thing you learn in the construction
business you start early like pop

used to say the first two hours are the most
productive hours of the day and even when he wasn't
in the business any more he'd be up before dawn
and he'd wait as long as he could stand it but

would finally just have to rouse me and i hated
getting up and that's why i never woke you
unless i had to but in my sixties and then
seventies i came to be just like him couldn't

sleep any more anyway so took to getting up
early and writing found i could get more writ-
ten in the two hours before dawn than
any other two hours of the day and so import-

ant it was to be writing so important
that was the thing that stayed
with me the longest you know
music and business and analysis and teaching

all these were passing fads but when i
finally gave up the writing i felt like quixote
at the end when he realizes he's defeated and
turns for home and he drops his shield and

sword and he lets his lance fall into the
dust and gives rocinante his weary
head to turn homeward
for the last time

there would be months
even years when i would
write nothing
but then

it would erupt again a flurry of late-
night typing fueled by desire by some
new illicit love for nothing fans the
flames of lust like immersion in

capitalism that wretched grind of daily
work leaves the body spent and the mind
empty and hungry and roaming the social
detritus like a famished dog though if

truth be told communal life
does the same thing even when i first
started in the business and it was just
me and charlie and dave renovating

houses in the day and playing in the band
at night and we'd come to work when we
felt like it eight thirty or nine and i had
one real carpenter josé who was from

honduras and he was older than us and
he always started at seven and if i didn't
have anything for him to do he'd just come
and sit in his van at the job until we got there

and then at three thirty and it didn't matter
if we were in the middle of something or not
we could be hanging a cabinet or have one
hinge morticed in a door and started on the

second but when three thirty came he would
pick up his tools and go home joe
we came to call him and he gave everyone
nicknames too like kirk he called cordón

because he was skinny and me he
called green giant because i was tall and once
wore a green shirt and every friday
he would announce as soon as we got

to work today is a good day he'd say because
do you know why? because today is mother's
day it was mother's day every friday he said
because if you didn't get your check you'd say

mother
fucker and when i'd get to work he'd always
say to me don't forget green giant today is
mother's day he thought he had to remind

me because back in those days making
payroll was sometimes touch-and-go and
thursdays were a big music night and
sometimes we'd be at the punk shows at jed's

till three and then i'd wake up at five
thinking jesus i've got three hundred dollars in the
bank and a fifteen hundred dollar payroll
to make i wonder how i'm going to

do it? and i'd go to the job and get them started
and then race around the city talking people
into paying me early and then i'd take the checks
to their bank not mine because the check

wouldn't clear fast enough i'd go to their bank
and cash it and they were often large enough
i'd have to go sit at someone's desk while they
called the owner to verify or sometimes they

would actually call another branch and have
someone look up the signature card and describe it
saying stuff like does the y swoop way down and
then underline the whole name? and then

i'd go stand in line and get the cash
and the teller would say be careful with all
that money and i'd stuff it in my side
pocket because it wouldn't fit in my wallet

sometimes it was five or six grand and some
weeks i'd be rolling in it and some weeks it
took every penny i had just to pay the guys
but the really remarkable thing is that i

never missed a payroll always managed it
one way or another those were sweet
days working uptown usually and the
crepe myrtles and azaleas all bursting with

color and the sweet olive filled the whole
town with perfume and we did good work and
the owners liked us and recommended us
to their friends and on some jobs i would

barely cover costs and some i'd make
a killing and that was just the way it was
even then desire raised its persistent head
and found me typing love poems

in the wee hours shaking sometimes with
the transgression of it for it would be some
friend of deb's or some wife of a friend and
sometimes the passion was shared and some-

times it wasn't and back then that made
all the difference and now it counts for
nothing for i was luckiest
generally when the poems made it

to the trashcan for on those occasions when
they went to their object and she
did swoon as intended
only grief followed your mother

put up with a handful it was
almost an understanding between us
though i didn't know that then
i couldn't see from up close how my

roaming fanned the flame of our own
desire how a hellish evening of accusation and
crying would end in frantic passion
but we can never see these things when

in their thrall love is blind
as they say but what they don't say
is that the whole world is
love

wretched blind love
fatuous hopeless stammering
misconstrued misrecognized love
even now it haunts even in paradise

i'd lay down happily in its illusion
its fictions of grandeur
i'd write it all again for who doesn't
like a good story? and is this

one any good? where
after all is the plot
the rising action where even
the characters except in snippets broken

shards of faulty memory
where are the unities and where
the moral? where the value
to the body politic of our fair

republic? where the catharsis?
where the bright light of truth? i give you
shadow-play on a cave-wall
muffled voices vibrations sensed from inside

the womb indeed it was an idyll
you were born into when we got to
new orleans in seventy five i looked
in the paper for carpenter jobs and found

one at pontchartrain beach drove out to the
job trailer at the amusement park sat
for my interview and the guy said how much
do you want and i said well i've got tools and

i know what i'm doing so i'm going to
ask for three dollars an hour and he seemed
to mull it over for a minute and then with
a straight face said okay and i started the next

day there were four of us on the zephyr crew
charged with walking the roller-coaster's route and
replacing any rotten pieces in the wooden
structure and we'd do that sometimes but if they

were too hard to get to or too high up sometimes
we'd just paint over them i'd never
ridden the zephyr and after that job vowed
i never would we would work until noon

every day and then sit down under the trees on
the lakeshore far from the super's shack for our lunch
and our foreman donny was his name had a stash
out there where he always had a bottle of

vodka hidden and we'd eat our lunch and
wash it down with a shot and then we'd
lay back and smoke and listen to football
and paul harvey on donny's little radio and the

guys would always nod when paul harvey
signed off and say yeah i like paul harvey
and i'd say i hate paul harvey and they'd look
at me like i was crazy at first and then laugh

and say something like oh your opinion matters
so much and then someone would bring out
a joint and we'd lie back and stare at the trees
and the clouds till four o clock when we'd

pick up the tools and go home and i'd only
been in town a couple of months when on a
gray rainy morning they told me there
was a hurricane coming and we had to tie

off the zephyr and i said what do you
mean and donny said somebody's got to
climb up there and he pointed up to the
highest part of the zephyr about ninety feet

up and attach guy lines so we can tie
it off the wind might blow a hundred
miles an hour tonight and i said sounds like
fun i'll do it and he turned to the guys and

said he says he wants to climb anybody else
want to and they all just laughed and he
gave me the end of a rope to pull up the
cables with when i got there and i put a

crescent wrench and pair of pliers in my
pocket and went out on the platform and
started up there was no walkway or stair or
anything you just climbed on the ties and it

was too steep to walk it like a stair but not
quite steep enough to climb like a ladder
so you had to go on all fours like a crab
and when i got about twenty feet off the

platform a gust of wind hit me and i had
to drop to my knees and from there i looked
up the track and from that view could see
the whole structure rocking in the wind and started to

realize what i'd gotten myself into and back
on the ground donny yelled you ok up there you want
me to bring you a safety belt? and the guys laughed
hysterically so i kept on going

and the higher i got the stronger the wind
and the more the thing swayed under
me and every so often i would have to stop
because my legs wouldn't move and looking

down was the worst because i could see
the track moving against the backdrop
of the buildings on the ground so i tried
to keep my focus off in the distance

down the beach or out to the lake it
was blowing up now with whitecaps and
waves to the bottom of the levee at the
back of the park and when i finally made

it to the top i put my legs through the
ties and started pulling up the rope i had
to pull up the two cables on one side and
then drop the rope on the other and pull

up those two and then bolt them to the eyes on
either side with cable clamps and i almost
dropped the wrench my hands were shaking
so bad and i looked down and donny and them

were slapping their thighs and laughing i guess
though i couldn't hear and i threw the
wrench at them and started down was never
so glad to feel solid ground though it too

seemed to rock for the first few minutes
and donny said come here and took me around
behind one of the sheds and pulled out a pint
of vodka from his back pocket and handed

it to me and i took a pull and he said good
job and then we all went home that night
was my first hurricane we just closed the shutters
on carondelet street and watched tv till the

power went out and then went to bed
it sounded like a train was passing most of
the night and in the morning there were
limbs and garbage in the streets but other

than that it didn't seem like a big deal
then i found out it had come ashore way
down in florida and all we'd gotten was
a little blow that was eloise back

when all hurricanes had women's names
i didn't work at the beach much longer
after that but got a job working on my first
uptown renovation this one for a lawyer

who'd bought a place on saint charles near
marengo i had no idea what i was doing then
i'd never worked on anything but new sub-
urbans and yet i was the best carpenter

on the job and it was good because i learned
a lot on that lawyer's payroll and i was working
with keith and joe and frank and beave and
even ralph worked there for a while but ralph

really wasn't cut out for physical work he'd be
cleaning up or something and i would walk
in the room and find him staring out the window
and it wasn't like i was really the boss or any-

thing but i guess i inherited pop's impatience with
that kind of thing and i got mad at him sometimes
he didn't last long there anyway and after that
the job started getting screwy

with the owner screaming at the
architect because the job
was costing about double what he had
said it would and one day the architect came

over to the house mid-morning and told us to
shut it down because the owner had quit
paying him and gone generally crazy the man's
an alcohic he told us and he took us down

to one of the po-boy places on magazine and
bought us lunch and said he'd call us as soon
as he got some more work and we had a couple
of beers and went down to acey's and played

pool for the rest of the afternoon and all was
fine but after a week without work i was getting
nervous deb had a job as a secretary for louis
roussel and only brought home about three

fifty a month louis was one of those old-school
capitalists that everybody hated and loved
he was famous for tearing down the saint charles
hotel he had applied for a permit for the demo

and a bunch of preservationists started lobbying
city hall and writing letters to the editor and
holding signs outside the building so one weekend
while the permit was still pending louis just

brought in a crew and tore it down nobody could
believe it and safety and permits gave him a ticket
and the city fined him a thousand dollars and he
paid that and then he cleared off the lot and turned

it into a parking lot and once while deb was
working there she saw louis fire one of his lawyers
the guy had gotten cold feet and settled a case
while the jury was out and then the jury came

back and awarded like a million more than he'd
settled for and louis took that lawyer by the collar
and pushed him out the door and threw his
briefcase after him and that scared deb pretty good

so she started looking for another shit job
found one eventually at bauerlein ad agency
and it was a young cute hip crew that worked there
kerry and kathy and devi kerry the dashing

young black yuppie and devi was gorgeous and exotic
from the south pacific somewhere and spoke
with an accent and deb started hanging out with
them after work since they went for drinks every

day and eventually started bringing home the
stories of how they all hung together at work in the day
and fucked each other randomly
at night or now and then in the parking lot

and we'd go to parties at their houses sometimes
which is where i met devi's husband ray
ray and i sat one night drinking scotch as he
told me how he was unsatisfied with the company

he was with and i said what do you do? and he told
me he sold roofing material but it doesn't matter
he said i can sell anything i'm just looking for a company
that's worthy of my skill and he told me about

some company he knew of that had been manufacturing
something and had figured out a way to reuse
some of the slag they had been throwing away and
so he said it was like they had found a way to make

profit out of nothing he said it was just brilliant
and i asked him where he met devi because he was
as white as she was not and he said he'd gone
to malaysia once for two weeks and that's where

he met her but he didn't really want to
talk about devi at that moment she was dancing
with kerry in front of us humping his leg
ray never even looked later i found out they

had some sort of open marriage and she fucked
anybody she wanted and would even bring
them home with her kerry told us one night
he fucked her with ray sitting in the next

room reading the paper the house quiet but
for the bed squeaking and her yelling
that image of him reading haunts me still
ray's last name was capowich and that's

what devi called him yes she would say
capowich will grace us with his presence tonight
most of that crew ended up in city government
at one level or another though i have no idea

what happened to ray and devi but as i was saying
after the ramoni job i needed work and got a call
one day from a woman named rose rose was
ralph's girlfriend at the time she was married and

it wasn't an open marriage like ray and devi so
the thing was always on the q.t. but we all knew
ralph was fucking someone named rose because he
was writing all these poems about her he had a

regular rose series going on and finally published
a book called hanoi rose and in it were things like
motherless gravity rose and apple-core choice land
rose and meeting rose but none of us had met her

so the day i got the call from her i said who is
this again? and she said rose you know ralph's
rose and i said ok and she said she had this friend
named penny whose husband wanted to renovate

his house and she had told them to call me
and she had told them that she said because ralph
needed a job and she wanted me to hire him
and i said does ralph want this kind of job?

and she said yes he wants anything right now
so i said well ok and sure enough this guy terrell
called me that night and he wanted to turn
his attic into a rec room and we did it for him

keith and i mainly and every friday afternoon
terrell would come up to the attic and pay
us in cash i would write up an invoice on
a scrap of wood or sheetrock and he'd pull

out a wad of hundreds and twenties
i asked him what he did and he said he sold boats
big boats he said hundred grand up
and i talked him into buying me a bunch

of tools because i said it would save money
so when i left that job i was pretty well
outfitted and ralph only worked there a couple
of days but it wasn't my fault there just

wasn't anything for him to do and
he didn't really want it anyway and one
evening soon after that he calls me and says
there's this new poet in town named maddox

we're going to the maple leaf if you want
to come and i went and met him skinny
and funny and smart he smoked a pipe and
drank martinis and we didn't know that

night in the maple leaf he would drink
and write his life away in that very bar
twenty years later but that night we went
back to his house and met his wife celia

and she was pretty and funny and
smart and flirted with everyone and we all
loved it they were living in the fitzgerald
house on prytania where f. scott stayed when

he lived here for a month in nineteen twenty
and we talked about how that was certainly
a sign of something though no one was quite
sure of what but for all that rette was poet through

and through and only wrote short
pieces he loved twain and fitzgerald and john
barth and he liked to quote barth saying
people say every novelist is a failed

poet but i say every poet is a failed novelist
he wanted to be a failed novelist but
in truth he wasn't he would sit for hours at
a time reworking twelve little lines typing them

out perfect on his selectric and every time he'd
change one little comma he'd type a whole new
copy so at the end of the day he had a stack of almost
identical perfect little poems and you could flip

through them and see a cartoon of the way the
poem had evolved like fast-motion history
and deb and i and rette and celia were a four-
some for a while when we moved to annunciation

street they moved a couple of blocks away on
constance and they called us one night and wanted
to do something but deb said ohhh we're already
in our bathrobes getting ready for bed and celia

said oh okay and then ten minutes later there was a
knock on the door and it was them in their bathrobes
and we played scrabble him puffing his pipe
the rest of us smoking cigarettes and we went to

the quarter one night before mardi gras celia and her friend
dressed as french maids and we sat in the window at
molly's on toulouse and drank till the sun came up
and the girls walked by saying hey baby where's

your harley? and we went to the hummingbird
for breakfast and over the eggs ran out of
stuff to talk about and rette says one thing
you know that's hard you have to pick

one thing to be and throw all those other
choices away and i said yeah i know what you
mean like when you think about your life you
see all these potentials but once you've done

something all those possibilities disappear like
they never were and he said yeah that's it that's
it exactly and we went with them down to mobile
for a weekend at the beach with celia's

family i don't think we ever got wet but stayed
in their trailer had martinis with breakfast at
the little thing on the bayou they called the yacht
harbor and played cards into the night

and deb and i lay in our little cubicle of a bed
and listened to them talking in the next room
celia saying i don't know what to
do i'm just so depressed and him saying i

know what you mean i can't seem to connect
with anyone or anything and she saying oh
you win you're more miserable than i am and
it wasn't too many years after

that when you guys were toddlers when he
called me from way down at the bottom of
a well he was losing celia and he knew it indeed
she had told him and i didn't know what to do

and so did the wrong thing tried to talk him out of it
but there was one thing about him and that was
he'd never be talked out of anything and he'd taught
at every university in town for one year each

and been booted from each for drinking
and after celia left and went up north with
a new man who actually made money and
took care of her and put her through columbia

he went through a succession
of shit jobs the best of which was nightwatchman
at the maritime museum and then finally quit
looking altogether and started living

at the bar sleeping where he could on the street
in a truck sometimes they'd just leave him on the
bench inside when they closed up and he'd be
there when they opened up the next day

seven years he lived on the street then in a
brief flash at the end started writing again
wrote on napkins and coasters and threw them
in a sack they kept behind the bar so that

when he died there was a manuscript of sorts
not the clean white things he used to type on
his selectric but these grubby stained castoffs
he'd picked up off the floor and the best of them

were as beautiful and as filthy as neon re-
flected in a wet street or in the gutter they
rose from and there must have been two hundred
people at the jazz funeral at the bar and ralph

read a long thing from yeats and maxine read
something about the plight of the homeless
and on the front of the stage almost un-
noticed between the banjo player and the

sax there was a box the size of cigar box this was
his ashes and we went over to fred's after that
and rodney jones managed to get the thing open
with a pop that sent a cloud of ash into the air

and down onto the carpet and we each
took away a little of him in a baggy
and next day they dumped the rest into
the river

and that was one strain one thread you
might say in the life of those years but there
were many threads you know it was almost like
what rette said wasn't true i didn't have just

one life but many you guys were a thread
deb was a thread work was a thread even
the band was a thread not for that long but
it burned when it was there it began when

charlie moved to town dave was living
in the front apartment on dauphine street
and charlie crashed there for a while
and we started jamming at dave's in-

sistence we'd play velvets covers and such
and i still remember the first day it hit
we were playing little queenie and somehow
on the ride it went where it was supposed to

and for the first time we felt what it was like
for the three of us to be in sync to be
in the beat and then one day dave and i
walked over to the church down the street

there was an old school building there aban-
doned and we knocked on the door of the
rectory and the maid came to the door and
went and got the priest and he got the key

and walked over there with us we offered him
twenty-five bucks a month and he said ok
we picked a room on the second floor but in
reality we had the whole building and we

screwed a piece of plywood to the door
and put a padlock on it and lugged our
stuff up there i found an old super
reverb and charlie had one of those

giant peavey bass rigs we were so loud the
neighbors complained for blocks around
so we hung some old carpet we'd demo'd
from a job over the windows and after that

the place stunk like a wet dog and was hotter than
hell in the summer and we'd blast away a
couple of nights a week and come out drenched
sit in the hallway and smoke a joint we wrote

songs and we'd write the song list and chord
patterns on the chalk board and we found a
lead guitar player also named bill and he took
us out one night to see a new band he liked called

sexdog and the next day we were driving in dave's
van and saw some of them on the corner and we
stopped and said hi and played them our demo tape
and two nights later they called charlie and said do

you want to open for us and charlie said sure
when? and they said in thirty minutes and we
went on stage at jed's breathless and after the first
song i thought i was going to pass out and had

to concentrate very hard it sounded weird up
there the sound got lost in the room and i would
play and a noise would come from somewhere
but it didn't seem to be me and the beat was

all off but nobody seemed to mind and we got
free drinks and stood at the bar and listened to
sexdog after just as flushed and high as if it had
been perfect and we had a handful of gigs after

that but nothing we did on stage ever matched
the practice room the whirling ecstatic
crushing roar of it the beat frantic pulsing
frightful feeding back and thrashing the

air and then dave was moving away moving
just to be moving he just got tired of new
orleans he said becky was pregnant and deb
said here you go moving away just when you're

going to have this baby so we won't have a chance
to get to know it and they packed up dave's van except
for his drums and the night before they left we
jammed and made a tape that forty years later

i'd listen to and not believe it was me playing
but next morning they drove off dave in the truck
becky following in the beetle and deb and me
and you in deb's arm and you in mine came

out and waved as they headed down dauphine
turned left onto louisa and went out of our daily
lives forever and i turned my attention to the
next layer for the motion was like a burrowing

a moving inward ring after
ring into the center the
singularity inside the
concentric selves

we needed to find you a school finally
settled on saint paul the lutheran place up the
street it was close and old fashioned
which despite our liberalism was what

we wanted and will
started there and ben
we took to an old indian
couple the mistrys just a block away

177

he was an architect who'd been forced
to retire because of cataracts
they were looking to take in
a couple of kids for daycare to pick

up a few bucks a week and mrs. mistry wore
saris and and taught ben a little hindi when he
was too young to remember and they had
altars to their god in the house and one day

they told us ben had eaten god's food which
they thought was hilarious and some mornings
i'd drop him and some mornings deb would
and he would walk through the gate with

an armload of lunch and toys and mr. and mrs.
mistry beaming on the porch and then we'd
drop will at saint paul two blocks away and then
we'd head off into the city deb to the law office

me to whatever job and deb was starting to think
about law school because it seemed like she
was doing all the work and they were making
all the money and i was taking mine a little

more seriously i was still playing sometimes but
no more charlie and dave working for me only
josé and a new kid named kirk and i liked them
and they liked me but i treated them like

employees and actually counted their hours
and stuff like that and deb went ahead and took
the l.s.a.t. and got into loyola and we thought at
first she'd go part time but when we looked

at it it was better to just do it as quick as
possible and she took out a student
loan and dove into it and i started getting
up earlier and earlier and bidding bigger

jobs and got my state license and incorporated
as william lavender inc. but when people paid me
i would ask them just to leave that inc. off
the check so i could cash it and pay the guys the

gross which made them happy and then i wouldn't
have to pay the withholding and the unemployment
and the worker's comp construction is
an informal affair half cash half on the books

everyone i knew in the business every sub did
business the same way they always wanted to
be paid in cash and they would walk around
with wads of it in their pockets on fridays

there were bars in the irish channel that
catered just to these subs and you could go
in them on friday and there would be a poker
game right in the front room with two or three

grand on the table and a bunch of electricians and
plumbers around it pete's bar had a window
so the black laborers could hang outside and
drink tall-boys while their bosses made or

lost their paychecks
electricians and plumbers
sheetrockers and painters and trash guys
i learned to trust no one

you just had to be careful about everything
or they'd take your money
and leave you with a mess you
had to spend more money to fix

and i gradually learned how to use the
cheap subs but not get burned and there were
some who were conscientious and took
great pride in their work some of the old

new orleans craftsmen plasterers and millshops
cal creighton for example whose crew always
wore white and who when he finished a sheetrock
job you could shine a flashlight down it and

not see a shadow and there was haydell who had
a sixteen foot lathe and i asked him how he copied
a column pattern and he said he would trace it
on a big sheet of paper and then stick the paper

on the wall behind the lathe and shine a light
over the stock and work it until the shadow met
the drawing and i knew how a lathe worked because
when i was in little league pop set me up with one

to make baseball bats and i made a bunch of them
and even though i couldn't play for shit the kids
who could liked to use my bats but
i'd never seen anything like this lathe

and that was my daytime life and at night we'd
watch tv and put you guys to bed and i'd play
guitar to put you to sleep or else read to you and
go back down and get out the dope can and

smoke a joint and then go to bed ourselves
and then when you were in about the
third grade you asked me if i sometimes
smoked marijuana and i said well sometimes

and later i told deb about that and she said
what? you told him we do? you have to tell him
no it could get around school and after that
she pretty much quit which was fine with me

it was a constant hassle keeping her supplied
and i got tired of dealing with it going over to
dealers' houses and they were usually coke
freaks just selling pot on the side we had

a good dealer named _____ for a while
he had a legit business like me and he always
had good weed at a good price but one day i saw
him on the street and his face was all swollen

and purple and he said two guys had kicked
down his door and come in while he was
sleeping and pistol whipped him until he
told them where his money and his dope

were and unlucky for him he happened
to be dry when they came calling and they
went away empty handed but really fucked
him up in the process and he got out of the

business after that and that left me buying
it on the street or from people i barely
knew and it started to seem like more
trouble than it was worth

or sometimes on weekends we'd go out with
deb's new law school pals and have sushi and
get drunk on sake or whatever and one of her
friends richard and i hung out a little bit went

drinking a few times once when i was reading
gorky park we had russian night and put a bottle
of stoli in the freezer and drank it all in ten minutes
then went to the quarter and got thrown

out of pat o'briens and shit like that we even
tried to pick up a whore but we were too
drunk to figure anything out and like i said
we were sort of pals outside of the deb connection

and he went into bankruptcy and construction
law like the big time stuff not penny-ante shit
like i was doing and he used to advise credit
card companies on how to get around bankruptcy laws

and once years later i
needed some advice and went to see him
on the fortieth floor of some building
or other and i said how

you been and he said well
what do you mean been?
doing ok i guess making about
thirty grand a month so i'm not gettin rich

but paying the house note got a nice place
in kenner got one of those new water beds that
feel just like a regular mattress nice bedroom
suite with a fireplace and everything very cool

so what can i do for you i assume you need some-
thing and i know you're not going to mess with me
like not pay me or anything like that and i said
oh no i don't need anything and i left his office

and went and got a lawyer i didn't know to take
care of whatever little problem it was i was
having and i never saw richard again and i say
that with some pride there were a lot of people we

dealt with in those days i was happy to never
see again there was for example george ackel
jefferson parish politician real estate developer and
general low-life we bid a job for him a build-

to-suit restaurant moving into one of his properties
and jimmy said it would be a great
deal for us because it was cost-plus and george
had all kinds of work and if we could get in

with this one we'd have it made but instead
of it being gravy it turned out to be shit because
george argued over every bill and we would always
have to end up settling so that instead of cost-

plus it became cost-minus and we'd go out
to his office in the back of his drug store in
kenner and he'd argue about the bill for an
hour while he took phone calls and put out

fires in the store and once a cashier
came back and interrupted us with something
about someone wanting their money back
and he flew into a rage said you go back

and tell that snot-nosed cunt she can sue
me if she wants and the cashier who looked
barely out of high school just stared at him
with her mouth agape horrified till he waved

her away with a disgusted gesture and i had the
pleasure of visiting him at his home once
we sat in the kitchen and talked but there
was a dog barking next door and he kept mentioning

it goddam dog fucking idiots don't know how
to take care of a dog and then while he was talking
to me he went to a little closet in the kitchen and
pulled out a pellet gun stepped out onto the deck

going here fido here puppy but he couldn't get
a shot at it as it was behind the fence so he just
said fuck it and shot out two of
the neighbor's windows george went on of course

to be one of the most successful developers in
the parish ran for office a couple of times and was
elected to the city council but he stopped short
of becoming a senator much as that would have

befit his illustrious career he left behind a
trail of disgruntled contractors and limited
partners and tenants and buyers and neighbors
and mechanics and yard-boys and secretaries and

lawyers and accountants but look down veterans boul-
evard today and see all those strip malls and
restaurants and bookstores and banks and
furniture stores and fast food places and

know that every one of them was built by
some captain of industry some
representative of the people like
george ackel and sometimes i'd think about

george about his big beer-gutted body moving
around the city walking from his office to his
car and driving somewhere and getting out and
yelling and getting back in sometimes i pictured

him out there like ubu
stomping around on his little stage
farting and declaiming his opinions on
matters of taste and governance

and i would go back to my office and go
over the books and try to figure out ways
to fuck him over to overcharge for something
but I could never mangage it he always won and i'm sure

died showered in comfort and attended
by white-skirted houris i'm sure he's here
with me somewhere now riding the
elevator up the concentric layers of

heaven for capitalism turns all the cos-
mologies on their heads you know reverses
moral hierarchy puts the godhead in the
asshole and the sceptre in the flame

and it doesn't stop at the strip mall either
turns us all into these things
i got out of the business mostly
just to get away from people like

george but i ran into him later in a different body
storming down the hallways of the university
waving papers and whining and railing
about the injustice of it about tenure and

pay scales below the southern average
why i've known poets who sit down to work with
the same set to their face that george had
when he aimed that pellet gun at his neighbor's

window the words like these will
fail and after a while you just say fuck
it and start shooting at the windows
shooting these words to you of the future you who are

the future the future
ferried across to this past i
have come gradually to represent
and in the end will have seen only

this coursing of languages among ghosts
and this ghost wrote the guest a letter
a sort of thank-you in advance and he dropped
the letter on the table like the key

i dropped onto the white tablecloth that day
i was forty and she was too
lunchtime in the restaurant of a hotel
downtown we each had a scotch and she

was saying it just seems so unfair just once
just once we do it and we get caught and now
we have to stop all that sneaking around and
it's all over in a day and i said hold on and got

up like i was going to pee but went instead to
the desk and gave them cash for a room and then
went back and laid the key on the white tablecloth
in front of her the heavy brass impressing itself

into the cloth and she looked at it confused at
first what is this? are you crazy? he's calling
me every hour and i said well you're at lunch
and she looked at the key and then looked

away out the window into the street where the
cars were edging their way down poydras and
the lunch crowd crowding down the sidewalk
and the corner of her mouth began to quiver

and curl like she was going to cry and she put
her hand to her mouth and spluttered but what
came out was a giggle and she sat there a moment
looking out the window and chuckling softly to

herself as if at some private joke and shaking her
head at the ill-fatedness of it all and i put some
cash on the table and said come on and we went
to the elevator said nothing on the way up

opened the room with its window on the grey
concrete scape of the city and she said wow
nice room and i was proud of her then that she
could carry her self-destruction with such aplomb

and also that the thing should become merely a
matter of bourgeois comfort a future of
rooms ranging nice to really nice and the
whole long past of envy and longing coalescing

like two axes the verticle and the
horizontal intersecting in that key
there is no need to go on with this story
its track is predestined formalized

built from a template but here
you get to hear
the great frame crunching
squeal of the ancient brakes

like that old ramshackle dodge i was
driving when you were born i paid
seven hundred for it when deb was pregnant
and we didn't have two nickles to rub

together i got the money from pop
deb was pissed but it was a good deal
and yes if truth be told i wanted a pickup
i didn't like driving up to the site in my

little corolla i wanted
a truck that could haul
lumber even if i never hauled any
lumber and she said so you had to get it now what

do you think we'll need it to haul the kid around?
and i loved it though it was a clunker and wasn't
very good for hauling it had no tailgate so when
i put stuff in the back it tended to slide out while

i was moving once i looked in the mirror and
saw a can of yellow paint hit the pavement
and a great ball of yellow liquid arc out of
it the cars behind me veered frantically i

turned onto a side street and sped up never
saw the outcome then one day a tourist cut
me off on claiborne and i got eight hundred
bucks for the insurance claim and just drove it

with a fucked up fender after that it rattled
and one cold morning it caught fire
leaves in the heater box smoke suddenly filled
the cab i had to pull over and jump out coughing

i took a hatchet and broke into the heater
box and put it out with a hose someone had
left conveniently in their front yard and ever
after that it smelled that wet smokey fire smell

like that house in fayetteville that boyd burned
down or like my amp always smelled after that
it had an automatic and a bench seat on which
you rode comfortably you could lie down and

sleep between me and the passenger door once i
got pulled over for an illegal left turn and the
cop came to my window but when he saw
you there asleep let me off with a warning for

you were so beautiful lying there he couldn't
conceive i could be less than upstanding
and it's true that truck rattling and
broken as it was and you in it and me

driving the city sweating covered with
sawdust in my tee shirt embodied an honest
proletarian pride carpentry is an
honest trade but i was too smart to be

honest for long and that truck saw the
end of me working with my tools and
the beginning of another era first running
a crew for eric eric taught me how money

works how the way you play the game is
you borrow on one project and then you
start another one and borrow on that one
to make it look like you're making a profit

on the first he would buy old houses in
the irish channel and evict the tenants and
put in lofts and cathedral ceilings and big
showers with skylights in them and we knocked

together shelves out of barge boards in the kitchens
and he'd put a sub-zero in it and call it the country
kitchen effect and he drove a mercedes and lived
on coliseum and he was always talking about my

percentage and how we would divvy up bonuses
at the end of the year and he hired a secretary
who had been a philosophy major and she became
my first dalliance i'd go by her place at five a.m.

before we went to work at seven and then i
started to like hanging at the office and my
carpenter friends started to drift away
keith was the main one he came in the office

one day after work and me and eric were
sitting there smoking cigarettes and drinking
scotch and he was covered in sweat and
sawdust and took one look at us and said

jesus this is rich oh and one more thing i
quit and he'd been my best friend for a while
before that and it wasn't too much later that
eric fired me he came out on the job and yelled

at me and threw some invoices in my face
and all the guys up on the roof and up on the
scaffold stopped what they were doing and looked
as i went to the truck and opened it up and

started throwing time sheets and dray tickets into
the gutter and he called me a few days later and
said hey we have some things to talk about why
don't you come in and let's be rational about it

and see what we can work out and i said ok and
came in and sat at his little board room table
with his little crew of superintendants and he said
well as you all know bill and i had a falling out over

some discrepancies with the lumber orders and
we're here to see what we can work out as far
as going forward and well i guess bill can speak for
himself so bill what do you think? and i said i think

you owe me a hundred and fifty bucks for truck
allowance for last month and he said that's all you
have to say? and i said yeah that's all i have to say
until you get me that check and he said laura would

you please cut bill a check for a hundred and
fifty dollars and my little girlfriend went out and cut
the check and brought it back and he signed it and
handed it to me and i got up and said see y'all

later and eric said but wait aren't we going to talk
about this and i said no i don't want to work for you
any more you're a sham and an idiot you're bullshitting
everyone at this table including yourself and i shook

hands with everyone at the table except him and
walked out and i never saw eric or laura again
but one afternoon not long after that i picked up a
six pack of dixie and went by keith's house after work

i sat in the truck and waited for him to get home
i saw him get off the bus and i thought he saw me
for my truck was unmistakeable and he started toward
me but stopped as if just remembering something put

his finger in the air in a gesture apparently meant for
me and turned around and went into the k and b
there by the bus stop he came out a little later with
one of those purple bags and walked on down to

the truck i got out and offered him a beer as he came
up and he took it and held up the bag and said i had
to pick up some important papers and he pulled out a
roll of toilet paper and i told him about

laura and he said oh i knew that was goin on
and i told him about deb finding out and he
hadn't known that and she and i had gone
for some reason in the heat of the argument

out to west end and we walked over the bucktown
bridge and looked down at the boats passing under
us and deb said as is usually the case with boats nothing
goes exactly as expected and keith heard that and

said phew and he moved back to florida soon after
that and that would've been that if he
hadn't come back for a visit a couple of years later
and he didn't even tell me about it but i heard and tracked

him down and made him come by the house
we were living on dauphine by then and
it was the first time he had seen ben and we
sat in the living room and talked after you

two went to bed and we talked about what
we always talked about books and such and then
he said you know i'm really glad you tracked
me down and made me come over here

i would have slipped out without looking
you up you know? and i said yeah i know
and just then i maybe even entertained the
idea i might have reclaimed him as a friend

but down deep i knew he was gone and he said
he was studying accounting in florida and then
he said you know the great thing about remem-
brance of things past is that you go through that

whole long thing all seven volumes and it is
only at the very end he reveals that all along he
was a flaming queer all through all those
confessions and revelations and yet he manages

to hide this one to the very fucking end
and keith walked out of the living room on
dauphine street that night and i never
saw him again and gradually over those

years of not hearing from him
and not writing to each other
his not writing began to rewrite the his-
tory of that era like in a movie you would

have a scene where the action hinges or
some primal betrayal is uncovered and the hero
or the anti-hero turns away and stares into the
distance and you feel the full measure of the loss in

an instant but in real life it doesn't happen that
way these scenes take decades to unfold they are
written and rewritten what was in the fore-
ground moves to the back and what was mere

detail becomes most significant like if you recall
that scene where i said good-bye to brazier and peacock in
vancouver well i stayed in touch with them for a
long time after that by phone now and then and

lots of letters written on yellow second sheets typed
on our smith coronas but then one night he called
me late we were already living on dauphine and deb
was pregnant with ben and i said hey what's happenin

and my heart beat a little faster as it always did when
someone i wasn't expecting to call called and he
said oh not much thinking about getting a divorce
what about you? and i said sort of the opposite having

a second kid did you ever think about doing that?
and he said oh lord no what kind of kid would i
raise? they'd be decadent probably suicidal and i said
well what's up with peacock why are you thinking

divorce? and he sighed as if with the futility of trying
to describe it and said she's just too dependent on me
she needs to live her own life and back then i was so
dumb i actually tried to talk to him about how to get

her out there living her own life and that might have
been the last time i talked to him sent letters and they
started coming back the phone number i had ceased
working i tried calling information now and then tried

under both brazier and peacock but never had any
luck and then just a few years ago i was talking to
ralph and somehow they came up and i said yeah i
wonder whatever happened to them and he said

well i haven't heard anything since maureen was
here and i said peacock was here? and i saw him wince
and he said oh shit i forgot you didn't know yeah she
came through town with some guy and

we all went over to otis's and i said you're kidding
was i out of town or something? and he said no we were
going to call you but she told us not to and i said really?
and he said yeah she said not to bother you and it wasn't

any big scene i just said oh and what was the news?
and he said she told them john had gone downhill
quit simon fraser without his ph.d. and was drifting job to
shit job and what was worse for him was he had lost his

good looks grown bald and beer-gutted it was hard
for me to grasp i couldn't even imagine him other
than skinny handsome suave and witty but thus
was that particular or actually two particular

histories rewritten it was like that map of new
orleans brazier drew for me my last night in vancouver
that showed canal and carrollton running parallel
and now i was learning it in periplum driving the

actual streets sitting at the stoplight at the
corner of carrollton and canal or in his favorite
bar molly's with the i.r.a. coffin hanging
from the ceiling those first couple of years in town

we went to the quarter all the time me and deb or
me and keith or me and deb and rette and celia
but by the time ben was born and we bought the
house on dauphine deb quit going and i would say

let's get a baby sitter and go out and she would say
oh you just go i don't mind and so i would go out
with charlie or dave or whoever to see a band or
drink somewhere uptown and i'd drop them off

at one or two or three and drive back across town
by myself and i took to driving through the quarter
driving right down bourbon the only street in town
still lit up choked with drunks and hawkers and

whores because in those days it wasn't just frat
boys and tulane girls with hurricane glasses it was
real musicians drinking after their gigs and punks
looking for action and the street awash in beer

cans and go cups and the neon flashing and the
girls in the doors of the strip clubs posing like
bunnies but bellies hanging over their hot pants
and the mannequin legs swinging out the window

of big daddy's and the absinthe house and the gay
boys on the balconies at pete's and the bourbon
pub and the real whores on the corners down
closer to esplanade and i drove through it like

that night after night with my arm out the window
and a cigarette just looking and honking the
drunks out of the way though i'd gone out of
my way to get stuck in it i always loved to be

lost in the crowd anonymous caught up in the
flow like my first mardi gras i didn't even know
what it was but we were living by chance half
a block off saint charles and on fat tuesday i

just wandered out and followed the crowd down
town gradually figuring it out how you were
supposed to catch the beads they threw off the
floats and stopped to buy a beer off a truck

and there happened to catch the eye of a girl
in a tutu and felt that breathless moment her
staring me staring and she broke it by taking
some beads from around her neck and putting

them on mine and i walked on through the
crowd as if in a trance and when i got to canal
and crossed over to bourbon the crowd as dense
as any i'd ever experienced and i just went limp

and floated into the quarter and there was a
girl stark naked on a balcony taunting two
cops who were trying to get to the door of
the building and someone kissed me and

i never saw her face but wandered through
the quarter and wherever i saw the crowd was
thickest that's where i went into the crush
sometimes actually fearing suffocation and

following the flow back down saint charles and
home and deb saying where'd you disappear to?
and i fell on her clutching and desperate and she
pushed me away saying come on now you're drunk

and don't really smell that good and i said ok look
i'll go take a shower ok? and i took a shower and
passed out and ever after that drove through
the quarter whenever i could just trying to

remember that breathless moment in the crowd
and it would be a long time ten maybe fifteen
years before i would pull over and open the door
and there was a time in my early sixties when

it all started to come back and haunt like this
one night i remember it was during the swine
flu pandemic of o nine and nanc and i had
both been sick off and on for weeks but we'd

gone out with some of the gang from school
for dinner and had a few glasses of wine and
alea my old boss was there and she was drinking like
i'd never seen her and we said where's your daughter?

and she said oh she's at the opera she went with
the third grade and i dropped her and they said
where are you going? and i said oh i'm going
drinking in the quarter and she laughed like

crazy and went back to flirting with one of the
new czech students and nanc and i cut out early
because i was afraid of getting sick again if i
kept on drinking and we went to bed early but

i woke up coughing about one and went in and
took some of my mexican codeine pills and did sodokus
until i fell asleep again and dreamed we were hopping
parties nanc and i like it was mardi gras and we

were at this house that was so crowded everyone
was sitting on the floor and no one knew each other
but everyone was friendly and tired and this girl
next to me even fell asleep and woke herself nodding

and i was tired too so tired i just lay my head in the lap
of a girl next to me i didn't know her or anything i just
knew somehow that would be ok and i rested my eyes
a minute and then said to her i hope this is ok and in

answer she bent down and kissed me and later someone
came up to us with a photograph of a float and said
his son was a welder and had made it and it was
right down the street did we want to come

and we all said yes and piled on as it started rolling
and we were passing all these people walking in
costume and people in convertibles heading to their
parades and i was thinking god how lucky i am

to live here and to have lived here like some people
only get to experience this once in their life but i've
been to mardi gras more than forty times think of
it more than forty times but the funny thing was

the street we were driving down to go to mardi gras
that street full of maskers was in fayetteville and
later i was back home and woke up and left nanc
in the bed and went into the next room and i was

just ecstatic sort of rolling around on the floor
remembering the girl who let me lay my head in
her lap and remembering the maskers but then
something moved out of the corner of my eye

and i had this feeling there was someone else
in the room and i looked and it was you will and
you were kneeling down at the bookshelf looking
for a book and i said will what are you doing here?

and i slid over to you on the floor and grabbed your
leg but when you turned toward it wasn't you at all
but someone else some guy with black hair and big
glasses and the guy looked at me impassively not

threatening but not friendly either just looked
at me as if i were furniture or something and i knew
then that i was dreaming and started trying to yell
for nanc to wake me up and i heard the noise

the actual noise in my throat i was yelling nancy
nancy but all that was coming out was a kind of moan
but she heard it and shook me awake and said it's ok
it's just a dream and i said i know and lay

there in the dark and i could feel the codeine
in my arms and i started thinking about how it would
be if there were no one to wake me up from my
nightmares how it would be at that last nightmare

when i would face the stranger and there would be
nothing to awaken to and it reminded me of a story
i'd heard a long long time ago a story from kay
when she was twenty she was working as a nurse and

had been assigned to take care of an old man i believe
she was just changing his sheets but she said it was
a struggle because he was disoriented and kept
forgetting where he was and that he wasn't alone

and he would start to jack off and she would
grab his arm and roll him over and he would look at
her like he'd never seen her before he let himself
be moved he rolled over like she told him but

as soon as she let go of his right hand it would
drop down to his cock again like it had a mind
of its own and we both went ugh and laughed
at this vision the masturbating auto-

maton and i vowed
of course over and over
that i wouldn't die
in a hospital but everyone

makes that vow at one time or another and one
day when you guys were in high school i think
me and mark were building some cabinets in
the carport on franklin avenue and we heard a

horn honk we didn't think anything about it of
course until it had been going maybe ten minutes
and finally mark went out to the street to see what
was up and he came running back and said bill can

you come help out your neighbor? and i ran out there
and it wasn't my neighbor at all just some woman i
had never seen who had pulled over to the curb and
her husband was in the passenger seat with his head

lolling back and his mouth open and he was that
gray color white men turn when they get old and
close to death and she was running around saying
joe oh joe and i asked her what was wrong and she

said she didn't know she was just driving along and
he was talking and then he just went silent and his
head rolled back and she turned back to him and
touched his shoulder and said joe joe come on

and i ran in and got the cordless phone and came
back out dialing nine one one and the woman had
opened the car door and now she and mark were
holding the guy up to keep him from falling out

onto the street and i put the phone in my pocket
and grabbed him under the arms and me and mark
muscled him out and lay him on the grass and he
was limp and fleshy and his skin like cold damp

clay and we lay him down on his back with his
eyes and his mouth open and his cheap poly
shirt bunched up around his chest and his soft
belly showing and it was like you could see his

whole life laid out beside him there some mid-
level bureaucrat wage-slave who'd sunk into a
meager retirement with his social security and she'd
worked a little behind a register after the kids

left and now their little house was paid for and
she kept it nice and clean and there were glass
figurines in the hutch in the living room and
the grandkids came over now and then and they

liked her snacks and they liked joe's jokes until
one day they started fidgeting in their
seats saying mom when are we going to go?
and then it was only the kids coming over because

the little one was at a friend's house or had soccer
practice or piano recital or homework or cheerleader
practice and i called nine one one back and
they said sir it is on its way and i said could you

maybe talk me through c.p.r. or something? because
i think he needs it but i don't know how and
she said no but maybe i can find someone who
can and she put me on hold and joe's wife was

kneeling on the ground beside him still just saying
joe oh joe and kind of whimpering though she
wasn't crying and mark and me standing there
feeling awkward and then the ambulance came

around the corner and i told the phone it was here
and hung up and the paramedics got out and
came up and you could tell by the look on their
faces when they saw him on the ground that

there was nothing they could do they were
kids about twenty-five they wore black combat
pants tucked into their boots and white polo
shirts and the one got down and did a half-

hearted c.p.r. while the other brought out a
breather with a squeeze bulb because nobody was
going to give this old gray guy mouth to mouth
and the paramedic said to the woman what is

his problem? and she looked at him like she
couldn't believe it and said what? and he said
what kind of medical problem did your husband
have? and she said oh i don't know he was ok just

a few minutes ago and the guy looked at her and
said nothing he looked a little bored really like he'd
seen this same scene already about ten times that
morning and they got out the gurney and

drove him and her away and after they dropped
them off probably cracked a joke and snorted
some coke and vowed never
to let themselves get that old

and there was the time much later
after nanc and i had moved to saint philip
one morning she was out
jogging on the bayou

it was early with
the grass still wet
and the fog rising off the water and she sees
something out there floating

turning in the water fifty yards off shore
and she stops and goes to the bank and
strains to see through the fog and sees a
shoulder break the surface and then a

bearded face and she yells once or twice
but the guy doesn't hear her so she jumps
in lands her feet in the bottomless muck of the
bayou and she's tripping over shopping

carts and brooms and bicycles and all the rusted
debris the city has thrown in over the decades
and though the water is only three feet deep
she starts swimming just to get off the bottom

and her sweat suit weighs a ton and her shoes
slow her down but she gets out to the guy
and she can see his weatherbeaten face up
close and he's just bobbing in the water not

unconscious his eyes are open and he's
breathing it's more like he just doesn't care
and she grabs him by the collar and starts
back toward shore has to push on the muddy

bottom with her feet slogging through the
shallows at the edge drags him up onto the grass
panting and spent dripping covered with mud
and he lies there like he's unconscious but he's

just staring at the sky and his eyes follow her
and there are people driving by ten feet away
from her on their way to work and they slow
down and look and keep going till finally one

rolls down her window and says are you ok?
and nanc looks up drenched and panting and says
do i look fucking ok? could you please call an
ambulance i just pulled this guy out of the

bayou and the woman in the car says ok i'll
call and she pulls out a cell phone and drives
away and when the cops get there nanc is
sitting on the grass beside the bum who is still

just staring at the sky and not moving but quite
obviously neither dead nor hurt and the cops
asked nanc what happened and she told them and
they looked at her with that same bored look

and then they radio'd in and ordered the ambulance
and when it came they took him to charity
and he never moved never stopped just staring
and nobody said shit to her after that

she walked home all wet and muddy and
told me about it and she said the main thing was
how nobody seemed to give a shit and later on
that morning i called the times picayune because i

thought they would think she was a hero and i got
a reporter on the line and told her the whole
story and she listened and took nanc's name
and everything and then she said wow this is

great thanks for the tip and next day we looked
for the story and there was nothing and the truth
was everyone was pissed at nanc for not letting
the bum drown the cops because she'd made more

work for them and the reporter because she'd
ruined the story by saving the guy there are
few things more boring than the near-death
foibles of the poor how do you imagine

a journalist would tell the story of that old bum
laying on the grass and staring at the sky?
i experienced all this first-hand of course
a little later but at the time it seemed news-

worthy the way dreams seem newsworthy
just when you are waking up but in a few
hours you have forgotten them utterly
and that forgetfulness caused me such

consternation for a while there i was so
terribly afraid i was going to forget every-
thing for years i wrote down all my dreams
in a database but then the software passed

the program by and i lost them all
it was no matter though because the real
exercise was seeing how much i would have
to lie to write the dream down or rather

how little lying i could get away with
and still turn those wavering ephemeral
threads into something concrete as if
writing itself were not as fluid and fleeting

a form as any as if to write were to build
something physical architectural that would
catch in the ground and hold while the river
ran by it was later on much later when

i woke up as it were and noticed what my
fascination with words had cost me eight
decades nine times nine years
gone in the twinkling of an eye this was

the prisonhouse of language
and there was a rape going on
one word in my mouth and one up my
ass and that great crowd of spectators

panting with word-lust thirsty for
the rhthymic orderly flow of
co and sub ordination those totally believable
hallucinations we call nouns the vapid

phantasies of the verbs the lilting
of prepositions the sweet nothings
of the articles those goo-goo i's
hungry for ofs and ah

what beatrice will guide me
out of this paradise?
which was she? in which body did she
reside in which face which mind?

i came to realize i had looked inside
a sufficient number of
minds and bodies
to know what was not there

but let me tell you lest any doubt
remain that hell of the divorce
years gave the lie to any amount of
huffing and puffing it's hard to be loverly

when you're crawling on the floor
of course there were those moments
playing kung fu with you two
in my new bachelor pad or

leaving for arkansas one night at two a.m.
bad fuzzy radio on the lonesome road
there is something about the promontory
that comforts and helps

and one day in that era i walked out the kitchen
door into the back yard on franklin and
the dogs were sunning in the glorious
spotless spring afternoon and i stared at them

for a minute maybe like years later that bum
would stare at the sky over nanc's shoulder
and i lay down in the grass
too lay down and curled up and felt

the sun on my back and sasha
sasha who was skittish and neurotic
because we treated her so horribly
sasha who never trusted us because she'd been

ignored too many times sasha whom
we never walked sasha who should
by rights have hated me and hated all of us
who if she'd had the slightest inkling of self-

respect would have run away and lived wild
sasha the siberian husky eaten up with fleas
that stubborn and steadfast sasha moved over
and lay down beside me lay down

with her back against my back
and told me something told me
not that everything would be all right
no the opposite

she told me everything was going to be
fucked up forever
nothing is going to work out and
nothing is going to get better

but this afternoon we are resting on the lawn
we are lying on the lawn
under the sun warm as a nest
and you'll remember this when you've

lived this long again
another forty years
and you'll be back here with me
resting in the yard

and remembering your future
sasha was
a casualty of the divorce
though momma-cat came with me

and buster went with deb
sasha got lost in the shuffle
discarded actually
and i never saw her again

and i'd feel bad about it
except that now i know
we let these things go
and in her doggy paradise

she's forgiven the whole fucked-
up world for the life it dealt her
not because she ever got any sort of
satisfaction and not because she

learned anything in the interim no
it's just because she let it go
and laid down in the grass in the sun
like me

for it ate at me you know
in what i thought then was my
old age but later discovered to be
my youth that is

in my sixties
after katrina and after the b.p.
fiasco i went around in a rage at
what the george bushes of the world

were doing to the planet
as that b.p. oil started seeping
into the wetlands it was like
the blood of the slaves come back

to haunt and i would lie awake
at night and the injustice of it
gnawed at me and i thought of
buckminster fuller

how he had devoted his life to
saving humanity all his designs all
his writings all his efforts all devoted
to this single incomprehensible task and if

you read him to this day you'll think
it possible even easy all you have to do
is plan and implement properly
designed structures but what this self-

less genius came to in the end can be
seen now at power boulevard and west
esplanade it's a mosque and i built it
somehow back in the eighties a group

of muslims got our name and asked
us to build them a mosque and we looked
around for the best way to build the dome
and we found a pre-fabbed geodesic kit from

a company that put fuller's picture on their
catalog and we ordered it and it was shipped
in on a truck and we set the pieces on the
roof of their crappy little building with a crane

and put it together it was made of
two by sixes compound mitered into
triangles and screwed together with a
plywood skin it was absurdly heavy

and on the outside we covered it with
regular fiberglass shingles and on the inside
we finished it off with sheetrock and that cheap
acoustic spray we called cottage cheese

and there it sat for years looking like
a strip mall with a dome on top and they
got their mosque for under forty bucks a foot
and they argued over the last payment just

like every customer did and if ever you
think that islam is a threat to the united
states just go look at how perfectly that
mosque fits in among the shopping centers

and subdivisions of kenner louisiana
if landscape and architecture affect cosmology
their houris will be from hooters and that
was the only geodesic dome i ever got to

assemble and so that was what
in my little ken
fuller's dream of earthly paradise came to
and for all those people sleeping

on the street? we could house them
but we're not going to
and all those children starving
in africa in india in china in america?

we could feed them
but we're not going to
and the whole big planet
teeming with birds and fish and mammals?

we could save it from the abyss
and all those species from extinction
but we're not going to
we can but we won't ought to be

our rallying cry the flag motto
for narrow-shouldered man
and when the last oil slick comes to shore
and the last bird sinks into the tar

last cipher in the geologic record
which there won't be anyone left to read
then lie down here with me here in
paradise

lie down in the grass and feel the good
warm sun on your back for
it is with all of us as it was for michael
that time we saw him after

his daughter's wedding
i was in arkansas to visit my
sister fayre who was beginning to die
as momma had and looking

more and more like her
she had taken pneumonia and when
she got out of the hospital they assigned her
to hospice which is if you don't know the

assisted suicide division of the medical
machine they just come by your house and
drop off whatever drugs you ask for
and fayre discovered morphine there in

her old age and we had the most pleasant
and relaxed visit she was saying
that she thought she was cheating the hospice
folks because she was getting all these

drugs but she wasn't going to die well
it turned out like the seventh seal for her
as for everyone you can't cheat
hospice but we were in this instance glad

for the morphine seemed
to agree with her she was relaxed but not
groggy perfectly lucid but all the old
resentments had fallen away she could

talk about her husband who had all
but abandoned her at the end
with no bitterness yes she said it's more
than hans can bear because you see

whenever i get sick he gets sick so
he can't come to see me now because i guess
he would die from it and she chuckled
at that and the next day nanc and i drove

to little rock and called michael's number
left a message on his
voicemail that we were passing through
and would like to see him if we could

and he called back a minute later and said
yes come on over we found him in the living
room of his little apartment off kavanaugh
eating a frozen dinner and listening to jethro tull

he still listened to the same music we'd listened to
in high school though he'd had some hard years in there
the family moved to little rock about the time
deb and i moved to new orleans and he married a

lovely girl named
georgie and they had
a daughter named her becca but
his family was struck with an axe

becca made it through high
school and went up to
fayetteville to start at the
university but was only there a month when

her boyfriend wrecked his car with her in it
she had to come home to convalesce
and never went back and gradually mike
started drinking like his old man had

going out to the garage and gulping
a pint of whiskey and then one day he
just moved out got a little apartment
and set about painting and spending

the bit of retirment money he'd saved
he painted pollockesque canvases
and discovered heroin he said one day he
woke up and the bed was covered in blood

and he didn't know why but he checked
in to the hospital and ended up being
there a month trying to rebuild his
liver but he'd come through all that

and now he was straight and living in
this little apartment off kavanaugh
with the walls covered with drawings
and canvases and through the whole

ordeal becca had been his mainstay he said
he'd told her everything left out not one
detail and she loved him uncon-
ditionally and his face got serious when he

said it and you could tell his daughter
was his all but then she'd gotten
married and the guy was an ass
michael had tried to like him and

when he couldn't do that to stay out
of his way and maybe the only thing he ever
withheld from becca was how much he
did not like her husband but this situation

began very quickly to unravel and one
night michael gets a call and it's becca
crying because the guy's in jail for d.w.i.
he'd run his car into a ditch and

the cops found him wandering in the woods
nearby and just by chance michael had a
little money right then because he'd just quit
his latest job and gotten a severance

check so he put up the thousand bucks and
got the kid out and becca cried and thanked him
but the kid himself was humiliated by the
experience and he started calling michael

and telling him becca didn't love him that he
was just a drunk and never did anything for his
daughter and that if he thought that thousand
dollars was going to buy him respect he could

think again and then becca would call him crying
and michael would say don't worry about a thing
he's a good kid i like him fine we get along great
and then he would hang up the phone

and seethe in hatred for this piece of shit
that the apple of his eye was so unfortunately
in love with and now michael was living on
unemployment and barely paying his rent

and becca and the asshole had gotten a seven
thousand dollar stimulus payment for buying
a house and becca had been saying that as soon
as they got that they would pay him back but

that stimulus check came and michael's didn't
so he asked about it and the kid said fuck
you i ain't paying you that money back you can
do one thing just one little thing for your daughter

you fucking washed up drunk and
michael lay in his bed that night
and all he could think about was
that kid's face under his fists

see this? he said and he held out his
knuckles so we could see how
red and scratched up they were
forty-five minutes on the punching bag this

afternoon he said and i saw his face with every punch
and i said michael you have to let it go
and he said i know that but i can't do it i can't
think about anything else haven't

slept a wink in three days and last night
you know i got down on my knees and begged
i don't know who i was begging to but i begged
to be released from this hatred

because you know if the kid was in this room
right now i would pound his face i wouldn't
have any choice but i can't let that happen
i can't do that to becca

and nanc and i got up to go
and he hugged my neck
said i love you
many a night after that i would

think of him
there in his little
apartment in little rock
down on his knees

heart open to that great empty sky
begging to be released from the endless
cycle of revenge
by which this earth is girded round

and many a night I would wonder
in how many other cheap
apartments in little rock
and in the little

world
were people on their knees
in how many countries
how many cities

working men and
working women
bankers politicians
beggars and thieves

crying the same ineloquent lament
not poems of heartfelt anguish
not songs of harmonic agony
words but not the words of the masters

for every woman and every man
will sputter like a babe
sending out their prayer to nothing
their petition to no one

and such prayers did i send
and some were sent through me
here in paradise
on my knees in paradise

for i was a messenger
a prayer wheel
remember that game we used to play?
the clock game we called it

you were about seven and you about ten
we had the pool in the back yard on franklin
it was circular and i would get in and
run around the perimeter in clockwise

direction until i had a current going
a kind of whirlpool
then you two would get in and attempt
to stop the clock

you'd stake a position and try to
block me or at least slow me down
as i passed in my diurnal track
but you were just kids and i

in my prime powerful in the water
i'd pick you up one on each shoulder
and trudge around like atlas
there was no stopping me

you'd huddle after each revolution
after each time i broke through
and dream a new strategy for
the next round

you might join arms and
encircle me like a gill net
but on every pass inexorably
i wiggled between you and got away

one of you might hold to the ladder
and hit me high while the other
went low and grabbed my legs
you might even pull me under

yelling and splashing suddenly
silent i would head to the bottom
slide under you and out the other side
breaching like a whale

waving fists in triumph
father time in triumph
butterfly stroke splashing hugely
then dipping under again pulling

through your legs arms your
faces in the bubbles then
silent again how long could i
hold my breath? i wanted you to

wonder so swam along the bottom
pulling into the shade
under the oaks gravel
on the bottom and

the great fish
kicking away
into the murk
and me kicking

holding my breath
sun breaking through
shaft alight
arm in motion hand

cupping the water
making current
not afraid
till breath run out

turning up toward
the full clear pane
of heaven
clouds skimming

and surfacing from this dream
i saw a sheaf of wheat
bound with flowers and garlands
the little girl with your face

hija de mi hijo
climbing up with a book
for me to read
fumbling for my glasses

i read green eggs and ham
and she said i am sam
i am that i am she said
and she closed that book and handed me another

and from a vague height i looked down
saw the old man reading
silent as if underwater
old man reading to a little girl

and what is he reading?
is it jonah and the great fish?
is it the highwayman? no it is
the story of the animals

see them pass two by two
under the proscenium
down into the valley
anteaters and bears are there

see the camels donkeys and elephants
foxes giraffes hyenas and iguanas
jaguars and kangaroos too
leopards and macaques and

nyala orangutan and panda come
quail and raccoon
snakes and tapirs also
uakari vulture and wallaby

all enter the clearing
with yaks and zebras
to be named by the human
to be written by the human

and she closed that book and opened an-
other and in this one there's a giant
a great hairy monster dripping
seaweed and oil

old fishnets and shipwrecks
hang off him
only one eye
in the center of his forehead

and the hero who has only his wits
must go into the cave
to retrieve the golden treasure
and he summons all his courage

and ducks inside
the beast
comes home
of course

and it stomps around
and breathes out a big sigh
filling the cave
with the smell of corpses

and it wrinkles up its nose
and it blinks that horrible eye
opens its wretched mouth
and says who's there?

and the hero answers no one

TITLES FROM BLACK WIDOW PRESS

TRANSLATION SERIES

Approximate Man and Other Writings
by Tristan Tzara. Translated and edited
by Mary Ann Caws.

Art Poétique by Guillevic.
Translated by Maureen Smith.

The Big Game by Benjamin Péret.
Translated with an introduction by
Marilyn Kallet.

Capital of Pain by Paul Eluard.
Translated by Mary Ann Caws, Patricia
Terry, and Nancy Kline.

Chanson Dada: Selected Poems by Tristan
Tzara. Translated with an introduction and
essay by Lee Harwood.

*Essential Poems and Writings of
Joyce Mansour: A Bilingual Anthology*
Translated with an introduction by
Serge Gavronsky.

Essential Poems and Prose of Jules Laforgue
Translated and edited by Patricia Terry.

*Essential Poems and Writings of
Robert Desnos: A Bilingual Anthology*
Edited with an introduction and essay
by Mary Ann Caws.

EyeSeas (Les Ziaux) by Raymond Queneau.
Translated with an introduction by
Daniela Hurezanu and Stephen Kessler.

Furor and Mystery & Other Writings
by René Char. Edited and translated by
Mary Ann Caws and Nancy Kline.

The Inventor of Love & Other Writings by
Gherasim Luca. Translated by Julian and
Laura Semilian. Introduction by Andrei
Codrescu. Essay by Petre Răileanu.

La Fontaine's Bawdy
by Jean de la Fontaine. Translated with
an introduction by Norman R. Shapiro.

Last Love Poems of Paul Eluard
Translated with an introduction by
Marilyn Kallet.

Love, Poetry (L'amour la poésie)
by Paul Eluard. Translated with an essay
by Stuart Kendall.

*Poems of André Breton:
A Bilingual Anthology*
Translated with essays by Jean-Pierre
Cauvin and Mary Ann Caws.

Poems of A.O. Barnabooth
by Valéry Larbaud. Translated by
Ron Padgett and Bill Zavatsky.

Preversities: A Jacques Prévert Sampler
Translated and edited by Norman R.
Shapiro.

The Sea and Other Poems by Guillevic.
Translated by Patricia Terry. Introduction
by Monique Chefdor.

To Speak, to Tell You?
Poems by Sabine Sicaud. Translated by
Norman R. Shapiro. Introduction and
notes by Odile Ayral-Clause.

forthcoming translations

*Essential Poems and Writings
of Pierre Reverdy*
Edited by Mary Ann Caws. Translated
by Mary Ann Caws, Patricia Terry,
Ron Padgett, and John Ashbery.

A Life of Poems, Poems of a Life by Anna
de Noailles. Translated by Norman R.
Shapiro. Introduction by Catherine Perry.

MODERN POETRY SERIES

An Alchemist with One Eye on Fire
by Clayton Eshleman

Anticline by Clayton Eshleman

Archaic Design by Clayton Eshleman

Backscatter: New and Selected Poems
by John Olson

The Caveat Onus by Dave Brinks

City Without People: The Katrina Poems
by Niyi Osundare

Concealments and Caprichos
by Jerome Rothenberg

Crusader-Woman
by Ruxandra Cesereanu. Translated by
Adam J. Sorkin. Introduction by Andrei
Codrescu.

Curdled Skulls: Poems of Bernard Bador
Translated by the author with Clayton
Eshleman.

Endure: Poems by Bei Dao
Translated by Clayton Eshleman and
Lucas Klein.

Exile is My Trade: A Habib Tengour Reader
Translated by Pierre Joris.

Fire Exit by Robert Kelly

Forgiven Submarine by Ruxandra
Cesereanu and Andrei Codrescu

The Grindstone of Rapport:
A Clayton Eshleman Reader
Forty years of poetry, prose, and
translations.

Memory Wing by Bill Lavender

Packing Light: New and Selected Poems
by Marilyn Kallet

The Present Tense of the World:
Poems 2000–2009 by Amina Saïd.
Translated with an introduction by
Marilyn Hacker.

Signal from Draco: New and Selected Poems
by Mebane Robertson

forthcoming
modern poetry titles

from stone this running by Heller Levinson

Larynx Galaxy by John Olson

The Price of Experience
by Clayton Eshleman

ABC of Translation by Willis Barnstone

Memory by Bernadette Mayer

LITERARY THEORY / BIOGRAPHY SERIES

Revolution of the Mind:
The Life of André Breton
by Mark Polizzotti. Revised
and augmented edition.

WWW.BLACKWIDOWPRESS.COM